Her Home,
The Antarctic:
The Royal Research Ship
John Biscoe

Her Home, The Antarctic: The Royal Research Ship John Biscoe

Trevor Boult with a
Foreword by HRH The Duke of Edinburgh

AMBERLEY

To all shipmates, past and present
&
to 'The Watch Ashore'

The author, by Alan Jones, electrical
engineer on RRS *John Biscoe.*

First published 2014

Amberley Publishing
The Hill, Stroud
Gloucestershire, GL5 4EP

www.amberley-books.com

British Library Cataloguing in Publication Data.
A catalogue record for this book is available from the British Library.

ISBN 978 1 4456 3860 7 (print)
ISBN 978 1 4456 3877 5 (ebook)

Typeset in 11pt on 12pt Sabon.
Typesetting and Origination by Amberley Publishing.
Printed in the UK.

Contents

Foreword by HRH The Duke of Edinburgh

BUCKINGHAM PALACE.

The Olympic Games of 1956 were due to be held in Melbourne, Australia, and I had been invited to declare them open. This seemed to me to be a good opportunity to use the Royal Yacht *Britannia* to visit various British Dependencies on the way out, and then, after the Games, to sail across the Southern Ocean to visit the Falkland Islands Dependencies Survey bases on the Antarctic. I was also hoping to be able to visit more British Dependencies in the Atlantic – the Falkland Islands, South Georgia, Gough Island, Tristan de Cunha, St Helena, Ascension Island and The Gambia – on the way to Portugal to join the Queen for a State Visit to that country. By some miracle this long and complicated cruise was a complete success.

The southernmost FIDS Base – Base 'W' on Andresen Island – was well into the Antarctic Circle, and as the Royal Yacht was not strengthened against ice, it was arranged that my party should transfer to the FIDS Support Ship *John Biscoe* for that visit. One of my guests on board was the artist Edward Seago. He was a compulsive painter and lost no time in painting a number of scenes in, and from, the ship. He also painted an evocative picture of an iceberg, which he gave to *John Biscoe*'s wardroom when we left her.

That was *John Biscoe*'s first season, and, as this book records, she went on to serve FIDS, and then the British Antarctic Survey, for a total of thirty-five years. This is an account of her life of service in the remote Antarctic, which enabled a vast amount of knowledge of that part of the world to be added to what we know of our planet. The author pays a generous and enthralling tribute to a ship which gave such unstinting support to the people who worked in the bases of the Falkland Island Dependencies Survey.

Introduction by Captain Chris Elliott MBE FRGS NI

The name *John Biscoe* is synonymous with British research activity in Antarctica. During the latter part of the Second World War a military presence was established on the Antarctic Peninsula. The operation was code-named 'Tabarin'. Although its real purpose has never been known, members of the operation made all sorts of observations, including meteorological, and recorded them. At the close of the war and the standing down of Tabarin, the then governor of the Falkland Islands believed that the stations opened for the operation should be manned and maintained for the continuance of weather observations and to survey the Antarctic Peninsula.

Thus the Falkland Islands Dependencies Survey (FIDS) was born. A ship was required to deliver the supplies to the Antarctic bases for a year. She had to be strong enough to sail in ice-covered Antarctic waters. On behalf of the FIDS, the crown agents bought a wooden, diesel-electric-powered ex-boom defence vessel, 194 feet long with a displacement of 1,000 tons. She was named *John Biscoe*. By royal consent she was privileged to be known as Royal Research Ship *John Biscoe*.

John Biscoe (1794–1843) joined the Royal Navy in 1812; he later moved to the merchant marine and became a British sealing captain working for the company Enderby Bros. The company encouraged its captains to make discoveries and survey coastlines while undertaking their principal task of taking seals. John Biscoe circumnavigated Antarctica in the *Tula* and *Lively* from 1830 to 1833. During this voyage, he discovered the coastline of eastern Antarctica, which was named Enderby Land. After recovering from the first part of this voyage in Hobart, Tasmania, Biscoe went on to complete his circumnavigation of the Antarctic, during which he sighted Adelaide Island, and named it after Queen Adelaide. As he sailed north-eastwards from Adelaide he charted two large islands, which were named the Biscoe Islands. He then made a landing on what was almost certainly Anvers Island and took possession of it in the name of His Majesty King William IV.

By the mid-fifties *John Biscoe* was becoming inadequate for the needs of FIDS. A nearly new small Baltic ship named *Arendal* was purchased and renamed RRS *Shackleton*. However, the expansion and operations of FIDS required two ships. A purpose-built steel vessel was ordered from Fleming & Ferguson Ltd, shipbuilders in Paisley, Scotland. This new *John Biscoe* was 220 feet in length with a load displacement of 2,200 tons. Considerably larger, she was fitted out to carry up to thirty-six personnel, in addition to a crew of thirty – scientists, cooks and mechanics, destined for the Antarctic bases. All those personnel were known collectively as FIDS. The ship had the capacity to transport 400 tons of equipment and stores, and also ample tank capacity for refuelling the bases. The new *John Biscoe* sailed from 1956 through until 1990, completing thirty-five Antarctic seasons.

The changes in the world and in technology over the period of the ship's life presented considerable challenges. That they were met speaks volumes for those involved and for the little ship herself. They say every ship has a soul, and it is true that some are remembered with affection while others evoke quite contrary feelings. I served as an officer on *John Biscoe* for five years and then as Master for a further fifteen years until she was paid off. I can honestly say that all the seafarers and FIDS whom I know are universal in their fond memories of this ship.

The maiden voyage of RRS *John Biscoe* for the 1956/57 season was particularly notable. It coincided with HRH The Duke of Edinburgh making a world tour on the new Royal Yacht *Britannia*. The *Britannia*, having departed New Zealand waters, arrived off the Antarctic Peninsula in January 1957. As the Royal Yacht was not ice-strengthened, Prince Philip and his party transferred to *John Biscoe* and visited several of the FID bases on the peninsula before transferring back to *Britannia*.

Nobody spoke of global warming in the early 1960s. Over this period the sea ice conditions were severe, yet, through valiant effort, the new ship generally managed to relieve all the bases. However, for one season she could not force her way into Marguerite Bay to get to the southernmost base, Stonington. The following season *John Biscoe* was assisted in her task by two American Coast Guard icebreakers. I recall being told that on one memorable occasion during this period *John Biscoe* managed to force on while the much larger and more powerful icebreakers were temporarily brought to a stop.

During this early period in the ship's life the Antarctic Peninsula coast was very sparsely charted. Hazards in the form of reefs and isolated rocks were numerous, position fixing was inexact due to poorly charted coastline, and difficulty was often experienced in differentiating between islets and bergs. The Royal Navy sent HMS *Protector* to the southern regions each season to maintain a British presence in the Southern Ocean. However, *Protector* lacked any ice strengthening, making it unsafe for her to sail any further south than the Royal Yacht *Britannia* had done some years earlier. *Protector* carried, among her complement, a team of hydrographical surveyors. For a number of years up to the 1966/67 season, these surveyors transferred to *John Biscoe* for a period of approximately two months each season to enable hydrographic survey. This work produced the first modern charts for the mid- to southern end of the west coast of the Antarctic Peninsula, thus enabling *John Biscoe* to undertake more safely the resupply of the bases. From then on, all hydrographic surveys were conducted from HMS *Endurance*, which entered service for the 1968/69 season, as she was similar to *John Biscoe* regarding ice capability.

When I joined *John Biscoe* for the 1967/68 season, Halley Bay base, situated on the east coast of the Weddell Sea, was being rebuilt. Halley II was to replace Halley I, originally built as the British contribution to the International Geophysical Year (IGY) of 1956. Halley Bay, remote from the Antarctic Peninsula, was normally resupplied by a charter vessel. The charter vessel at the time was *Perla Dan*. As she could not accommodate all the personnel required to complete the rebuild, *John Biscoe* was also programmed for that season to go to Halley. Satellite imagery was just beginning at this time. The headquarters of the British Antarctic Survey (BAS) received satellite images of Weddell Sea ice and passed this information on to the ships. *John Biscoe*'s captain, heeding the information, arrived at Halley some days ahead of *Perla Dan*, despite having sailed from South Georgia a number of days after *Perla Dan* had departed.

By the late 1960s the usefulness of inflatable craft was being realised. The RNLI had developed and modified such craft for inshore rescue. Two ex-RNLI 16-foot inflatables powered by 40-hp engines were added to *John Biscoe*'s outfit. Scientific staff soon appreciated the value of these craft as a means of ship-supported coastal survey for geology, biology and botany. The time that had been devoted to hydrographic survey the previous season was now used for ship-supported landings around South Georgia and South Orkney, and on the Antarctic Peninsula, in support of various scientific disciplines.

In 1967 BAS became a component of the Natural Environment Research Council (NERC). One outcome of this was the agreement that a new purpose-built logistic supply vessel should be built and the RRS *Bransfield* came into service. She replaced both the *Shackleton* and the annual charter ship for the Halley relief. *Bransfield*'s capabilities were such that *John Biscoe* was relieved of many of her previous logistic commitments, thus freeing up more time for ship-borne science. In 1979, *John Biscoe*, having supported offshore biological science and oceanography in the late 1970s, underwent a major refit and conversion to a marine biological and oceanographic research ship, while also maintaining a degree of logistic supply capability.

From the early 1970s *John Biscoe* spent approximately six weeks and sometimes longer each season supporting ship-borne biological research. This commenced with benthic surveys around South Georgia and, from 1978, operations for the Offshore Biological Programme (OBP). Every season the ship was programmed to undertake approximately three months of biological and oceanographic research. This included one winter cruise. The BAS OBP scientific cruises carried out on *John Biscoe* gave BAS a preeminent position and authority, which led to the signing of the Convention on the Conservation of Antarctic Marine Living Resources (CCAMLR). This agreement regulates fishing south of the Antarctic Convergence, based on the evidence from marine biologists.

The experience gained on *John Biscoe* was of great value when her replacement RRS *James Clark Ross* was designed. *James Clark Ross* has proved to be a first-class research ship, much sought after by the international scientific community.

The proximity of the Falkland Islands to the Antarctic Peninsula, Weddell Sea, South Sandwich Islands, South Georgia and South Orkneys led to the administration of those regions becoming the responsibility of the Falkland Islands Governor, hence the name Falkland Islands Dependencies (FIDS). When the Antarctic Treaty was signed in 1961 it was agreed that all territorial claims on Antarctica would not be pursued, but held in abeyance. The British Antarctic Territory was in consequence administered directly by the Foreign and Commonwealth Office in London and removed from FIDS; FIDS became BAS. This change did not alter the routing of the ships; the Falkland Islands remained, and remain to this day, an ideal 'jumping-off point' to Antarctica, supplying bunkers, fresh provisions and personnel changes.

For all members of BAS, and perhaps especially for ship's staff, the Falkland Islands became a second home. In 1977 *John Biscoe* arrived in Stanley shortly before Christmas, part way through the Antarctic season. Our call was seized upon by the manager of the Falkland Islands Company, as their vessel had suffered major engine failure. This meant that wool had not been collected from the farms and brought into Stanley to be loaded on to a charter ship for transportation to Europe. 'Could *John Biscoe* sail around the islands to collect the wool and bring it into Stanley?' The Falkland Islands' Governor made a formal request to the director of BAS and, after certain safeguards such as insurance were sorted, I was given leave to proceed. I embarked a local captain, Jack Sollis, as pilot; he was a man who knew the coast and harbours like the back of his hand. We visited five farms and loaded in total about 250 tons of wool, arriving back in Stanley on Christmas Eve.

I have highlighted some of what may be called the 'extracurricular' activities of *John Biscoe*. I should point out that from her first season up to the first season of *Bransfield* in 1970/71, *John Biscoe* was the primary ice-strengthened ship. The principal task was the relief of the numerous bases in Antarctic waters, taking supplies and facilitating personnel changeover. She would lay depots on remote islands to allow parties to travel by dog sled once the sea ice formed in the winter. Another task (which ended in the early 1970s) was to take seals to feed the dogs – a process which also benefited scientific research on the seals themselves.

The author, Trevor Boult, joined *John Biscoe* on her final voyage to Antarctica, her thirty-fifth season south. In this book he recalls his impressions and describes life on board. This account will give the reader an insight into shipboard life and the ethos that prevailed, not only on the ship but also throughout BAS, both on the bases and back in headquarters in Cambridge. Trevor has written many published articles on ships in various trades, and documented the life of craft such as the light vessels and tenders of Trinity House, the Norwegian coastal ferry service, and the Royal Mail Ship *St Helena*.

The UK has been at the forefront of scientific endeavour in the Antarctic. Ships are essential tools to carry this out. Global warming has made everyone far more aware of our environment; the research carried out in Antarctica is now frequently in the news. The life and times of *John Biscoe* really pre-dated this greater awareness. However, but for the work carried out by BAS, supported by this little ship, the UK's pre-eminent position in the worldwide scientific community would not be.

I think it very fortunate that Trevor joined as third officer for this final voyage. He is one of the rare officers who make a hobby of writing, and thus recorded for posterity part of our maritime heritage.

Captain Chris Elliott, MBE FRGS NI

Preface

'Trevor, British Antarctic Survey is on the phone. They have an offer which might interest you.' The Marine Personnel Manager of Research Vessel Services, in his office overlooking Barry Dock in South Wales, took in my less than glamorous but typical workaday attire of rust-stained boiler suit and worn boots, typical of a Merchant Navy deck officer standing by an operational ship in port.

Anticipating the subject of the conversation, and wearing a look of amusement, he handed me the receiver. I was connected to his counterpart at the British Antarctic Survey's headquarters in Cambridge. My proposal of a year previously had been remembered; that of sailing as a photojournalist on their classic and quietly renowned ship *John Biscoe* during her work in Antarctica, in support of the British scientific bases. The idea had found favour but, as cabin space on the little ship had been at a premium, there would sadly be no room.

'We have a one-voyage vacancy for an officer on the *John Biscoe*. The regular man will be standing by at the completion of her replacement – the *James Clark Ross* – at Swan Hunters, on Tyneside.' As my jaw had evidently slackened at the extraordinary opportunity, my employer sitting opposite openly broke into a smile. Such a secondment would need his approval and a release from my schedule of work on the Government oceanographic ships of the Natural Environment Research Council.

He agreed; I accepted. For me at least it was to become the product of personnel management at its best and quite literally a trip of a lifetime, as both observer and active participant on the last and final voyage in Antarctica of the Royal Research Ship *John Biscoe*.

CHAPTER 1

A Welcome to Antarctica

From home to Brize Norton airbase – Ascension Island – arrival at the Falkland Islands – John Biscoe – Montevideo – to the door of Antarctica.

Accepting a rented Ford Escort, delivered on 10 December 1990 to my home in north-east England, seemed a parochial way to begin a winter journey that would, eventually, lead to standing among skidoos and a caterpillar-tracked personnel tractor on the remote and pristine autumnal snow slopes at the scientific base of Rothera, deep in the British sector of the Antarctic. These two locations were to mark the furthest north and south of my coming association with the RRS *John Biscoe*, and the many people with whom I would meet and work in the common endeavour of furthering knowledge about the most alluring and mysterious of continents.

Professional mariners and their loved ones carefully make light of departures and the latest prospect of a lengthy and self-sufficient separation. Five months would pass before the unrestrained joys of homecoming. Constraints on luggage space meant that only tiny tokens could be packed, to be opened on Christmas morning in the height of a far-distant Antarctic summer.

The day's final destination was to be RAF Brize Norton in Oxfordshire, but the route was to be indirect. In a homely cottage kitchen in a rural village gem of Northumberland, I made first acquaintance with Hamish, newly appointed as *John Biscoe*'s catering officer. We had to continue westward to Carlisle: I had a necessary appointment with a needle, for a yellow fever vaccination.

It was with a feeling of some relief that we could finally start heading southwards. The earlier television images of the previous day's heavy snowfalls preoccupied our journey with uncertainties. It was imperative that we make the special flight that would take us all the way to the Falkland Islands.

Entrance security at Brize Norton confirmed that the flight was due to board at midnight. Gifted with time to spare, it was no hardship to sample an ale at a village hostelry nearby, as something of a toast to the native soil from which we were shortly to take our leave.

The Irish lilt, warm smile and friendly handshake came as a delightful surprise and icebreaker that would prove to be so typical. 'I'm Maurice, radio officer of the *John Biscoe*. I've brought your special clothing issue through from Cambridge.' Accompanying him were the second engineer and three GAs – general assistants – an understated term for specialists in polar survival who would assist scientists at temporary tented field stations, set up in demanding locations in the Antarctic and left for lengthy periods to fend entirely for themselves.

It was cold, damp and pitch black as we boarded the British Airways Tristar. The flight was essentially for military staff but with facility for civilian travel. After eight hours the aircraft approached Ascension Island, in intense morning sunshine. This strategic British dependency is home to the American airbase of Wideawake, a somewhat incongruous name to those surfacing from the dubious sleep of a long-haul flight. Named after the sooty or Wideawake terns that breed in great profusion on the island, it boasts one of the longest runways, which is no mean feat, closely flanked as it is between steep-sided and cinder-like volcanic mountains.

A temperature of some 25° greeted us on our disembarkation. Politely but definitely herded into a pleasant open-air compound by escorts from the airbase, the gates were discreetly locked for the ninety-minute duration of refuelling. Copious liquid refreshments were needed to combat the shock of seasonal adjustment from dim and drizzly coldness to a dazzling dry heat.

It was a further eight-hour flight to East Falkland and the airport at Mount Pleasant. The base was a huge uncompromising complex of green warehouse buildings. In mid-afternoon we set foot on that distant land which had suffered a particular conflict in the recent past and where its echoes still reverberated. All travellers, whether military, civilian or holidaymakers, were given a talk by the Army about minefields. We were shown a range of ordnance which might be encountered underfoot, and advised of the need to use updated minefield maps. With barrack-room humour we were uplifted with the order 'enjoy your stay'.

The one-hour journey by coach to Port Stanley took us across low undulating countryside, displaying mainly a wiry grass of monotonous brown and an occasional ridge or isolated peak of grey slab-rock. The variously coloured small buildings of Stanley eventually offered a stimulating contrast to the otherwise drab landscape. Across the expanse of Stanley harbour a large stern trawler lay alongside. In a further inlet, a Royal Fleet Auxiliary was moored. Port Stanley jetty lay east of the town, supporting a fortress of steel warehouses.

At the pier-end could be glimpsed the assertive red and white of a small ship, diminutive beneath a massive sky but assuredly at home in her setting. I savoured my first view of *John Biscoe*.

The coach drew up within yards of the gangway at the ship's stern. Beneath the name, her port of registry – Stanley FI – confirmed that indeed she was very much at home. Like any other mariner about to set foot aboard an unknown ship, a critical eye was cast upwards to absorb first impressions of the next workplace and home from home. *John Biscoe*'s lines were sweet and traditional. She exuded a palpable charm which overlay an indomitable history of thirty-four years of service in a superlatively testing sphere of operations. The shore leave board indicated that departure was to be at 19.00 on the same evening. So much for a night alongside for the weary globetrotting travellers who were hoping to adjust and catch up on sleep!

Appropriately, my first meetings were with the chief officer and John, who was relinquishing his position as third officer to me, and taking over from a colleague as second officer. In his friendly London twang he intimated that dinner was imminent and that dress uniform was required. Performing a quick change is as desirable a trait for a seafarer, as it is in the theatre. A late glance in a mirror hinted that two-day stubble would not do, prompting a hurried inauguration of the cabin sink for a shave. The lethargy of travel had snapped into a shipboard discipline, yet mellowed by that stalwart of English country life – the World Service broadcast of *The Archers*.

I approached the wardroom with anticipation and some trepidation. There was to be formality and new faces; I was a new face and an unknown quantity. Yet it was a familiar countenance I first saw, from my interview at Cambridge: the disarming and welcoming master of *John Biscoe*, Captain Chris Elliott.

Clustered around the radiant glow of the electric fire in its imposing mantelpiece setting, graced by an Edward Seago oil painting of the ship in her working environment of ice, several people sat lounging in luxurious armchairs. I was introduced and, with annoying certainty, instantly forgot their names. With reassuring drink in hand and the prospect of a fine meal ahead, I became more aware of the expansive yet homely feel to the room, which spanned the full width of the accommodation. Wood panelled, carpeted, decorated with crests, paintings and inspiring polar photographs, the scene was completed by the settings of the two long dining tables to which we were gently summoned by the gong, at the invitation of Shaun the steward, who was also 'keen to get off on the right foot'.

The place settings were precise, the cutlery of quality. I had a proper napkin in its own embossed silver ring. Newly joined fellow travellers were transformed into fresh figures, for an instant unfamiliar in their own neatness and formal attire. We evidently all scrubbed up well.

Sated and refreshed, and with my first four-hour watch to do that night, I joined John on the bridge to help test and set up the equipment before sailing, and generally familiarise myself with what would be my 'office' between the hours of 8 a.m. and midday, and 8 p.m. and midnight, when the ship was at sea, in the role of navigator and watchkeeper. I was impressed by its light and spacious airiness, the neat, simple, uncluttered and well-planned layout, unlike so many bridges of more modern ships in the era before integrated systems, where generations of stand-alone equipment led to ungainly and fragmented ergonomics.

A central and set-back traditional steering telemotor sported a gleaming brass wheel of generous size; a foot grating stood on the laid wooden deck. The large windows offered excellent forward visibility, not only elevated above the low well deck, but to enhance the judgements and careful manoeuvrings in many states of sea ice. High on the foremast a substantial crow's nest cradled an imposing down-slanting searchlight, as an occasional but vital night-time probe into the unforgiving darkness ahead.

In the other departments all was being prepared for a departure for sea. It was with a long-practised ease and lack of any ceremony that the mooring lines were slipped. As the in-hauling anchor pulled the bow away from the berth, and the rapid ringing of the bell forward indicated that the anchor was aweigh, Capt. Elliott conned the ship by hand tiller and engine control, aiming her across the harbour towards the rocky narrows. Two leading marks on the far shore were brought into line to safely negotiate the defile. Surging into the outer inlet of Port William, a graceful arc put the open sea ahead. Clearing the headlands of Cape Pembroke and Mingeary Point, a northerly heading was set for the 1,000-mile passage to Montevideo in Uruguay, for well-earned R-and-R, rest and recuperation – most of the crew had already spent several busy months on the ship, since her departure from the North Sea port of Grimsby the previous September.

Thus, on her northerly heading I had found her, taking over to start the first of many extraordinary bridge watches. Invigorated into life aboard sooner than I had anticipated, I suppressed a certain childlike excitement. I had already fallen completely for the ship, and what she represented.

It was a grey evening with a brisk wind from the south-west. Recumbent and without detail, it was not difficult to imagine the retreating land as Scottish islands. The long flight south had given no real sense of covering distance. It was therefore novel to be using and thinking in terms of southerly latitudes. The emphatic position on the satellite navigation screen was a significant change: 51° south, 58° west. What had been the approach to the north's shortest day had become the herald of the longest day, a leap from winter to summer.

The need for another mental adjustment, a reversing of applied principles, became obvious. In weather terms, in the southern hemisphere winds circulate about high- and low-pressure areas in the opposite directions to those north of the equator. I made a mental note to watch which way water spiralled out of the sink. On the latest facsimile weather map, the onion rings of a depression were prominent. Contrary to northern expectations of a headwind, the actual attendant breezes remained helpfully astern for much of the voyage, the accompanying sea and swell allowing a speedy and comfortable passage.

The bridge was a place to savour. It was quiet, without the necessity for distracting radio traffic. It functioned without the need for either compromise or multitasking, and was the rightful place to exercise the arts and science of practical navigation. The open bridge-wings were to become exclusive balconies to the play of natural elements, as much to feel balmy breezes or chilling blasts spilling over the dodgers as to take sextant sights; to watch tobogganing penguins or to listen intently to the ominous rasp of waves surging at the foot of icebergs hidden within the clammy embrace of fog. I discovered the luxury of having a permanent lookout, not only by official obligation during the hours of darkness but also in the daytime. As the ship had no automatic fire alarm system, the seaman lookout also carried out hourly patrols of the ship, and catered for the watchkeeper's beverages.

It was with some satisfaction that I took to my bunk after midnight, the first real chance I had had to acquaint myself with my cabin. A workmanlike hum came from the engines; gentle creaks became the lullaby of contented normality.

* * *

John Biscoe was a Voluntary Reporting Vessel for the British Meteorological Office. They supplied the ship with special equipment and stationery to observe, record and relay specific weather data. The task was well supported, with observations being taken and coded for transmission every six hours, then sent by the radio officer to British Antarctic Survey stations and the UK. One of the additional duties of the third officer was principal observer, responsible for the equipment, record-keeping and in ice conditions to prepare ice charts. It was to become a mark of pride for all the observers not to miss any scheduled observation. The entries made in the Met. Logbook, with its wide format and close-packed rows of esoteric code numbers, slowly marked the passage of time. Aware that this would be the ship's final record, a neat copy kept pace with its working counterpart. This painstaking task was ultimately to lead to official recognition by the Met Office.

The Navigation Department's Deck Logbook was a hefty tome, weighed down by its myriad matter-of-fact entries of the days' events, but devoid of the diverse dramas or delights behind many of those entries. Every morning the bosun's mate took soundings of the tanks, bilges and other spaces, transferring these into the Sounding Book and to the chalkboard in the chartroom. As a regular clerical task for the third officer, these figures were entered into the Deck Log, together with oil figures taken periodically from the Engine Department.

At noon, when the bridge watch was handed over to the second officer, came the daily strident testing of the ship's whistle, and a check on the manual steering, reverting briefly to the oft-polished wheel for a turn to port and starboard before returning to the auto setting. The two officers then opened their workbooks, separately calculating the noon figures, to double-check and agree. On the long steady course northwards, the Day's Run calculation was made simple by a navigational calculator. From the final figures, noon chits were filled out and presented to the captain, chief engineer and radio officer. In the crew alleyway, a Perspex-protected chart showed the ship's position and adjacent, in red chinagraph, a breakdown of the distance, course and speed made good, and the estimated time of arrival at the next destination.

The evening watch brought with it an invigorating coolness. After twilight had passed and the sky had become properly dark, many of the stars appeared to shine with the intensity of planets in a northern sky, and in fresh configurations to ignite curiosity and wonder. Familiar to the north-west lay Orion, and the Pleiades.

* * *

Midway between the Falklands and Uruguay, wandering albatrosses appeared, distinguished additions to the regular birds: black-browed albatrosses and cape pigeons. Conditions had become warmer. Thankful that the fresh breeze had stayed in the south-west, we were all aware of how different both speed and comfort would have been if heading the opposite way. Minds were cast thoughtfully ahead to the 1,700-mile journey southwards, across the unpredictable Drake Passage to the tip of the Antarctic Peninsula, and our schedule at James Ross Island.

On the second day, ship's clocks were advanced by an hour, to align with the time at Montevideo. To share out the lost hour, each of the three watch periods worked twenty fewer minutes.

Below decks, the GAs filled their time with preparations and exercises. They carefully went through the issues of drugs and medicines with the ship's doctor, and practised giving each other injections, but with only water in the syringes. Curiosity found them having a guided tour of the bridge. The chance to plot a position on the chart seemed a desirable bonus.

Through subtle changes the wind had swung round until nearly ahead. Opposing the swell, which still bowled northwards, the fresh wind-waves ran past from bow to stern, giving the illusion of our making rapid speed. Through it all the ship forged with an effortless and sea-kindly grace. By the evening of the third day *John Biscoe* was 50 miles east of Mar del Plata, closing gradually on the coast.

Approaching Rio de la Plata – the huge bay and outfall of the River Plate – the sea colour changed from its oceanic hue to the caramel brown of the silt-laden shallows. With the echo sounder graph running, the depth trace slowly rose until it indicated only a few metres' depth beneath the keel. Such proximity to the seabed can have undesirable effects. Engine exhaust temperatures can rise in sympathy with demands on horsepower. On the bridge control console an eye was kept on the gauge, the speed being adjusted if the needle crept up to the 1,600 shaft-horsepower limit.

The passage had gone by without sight of land, and no other shipping save a few distant fishing boats. Land was initially detected by radar. The first tentative echoes conformed to the basic charted shape of high ground and headlands at Montevideo. Despite the luxury of regular satellite navigation positions, the radar still provided a seamanlike confirmation and the means of assessing position when required, rather than solely at the schedule of satellite fixes. Throughout the voyage their pattern showed the ship's track to be varying, under the influences of changing winds, ocean currents and tidal streams. At the watchkeeper's judgement, small course changes were made to counter these effects, to help maintain the approved track and to keep to the required course-to-make-good. All such adjustments were recorded in the Deck Log. Direction was determined by both an electrical gyro compass and a marine magnetic compass. The accuracy and errors of both were regularly determined and recorded.

More blips began to appear on the radar screen, representing individual vessels within detection range but as yet not visible to the eye. The radar screen was shielded from daylight by a truncated cone of a hood. At the top, a contoured rubber face-opening completed the seal. Flapped hand-holes at each side enabled manual access to the screen. Because it was an older generation of radar, which displayed only raw, as opposed to processed, data, targets had to be hand plotted to assess their potential for collision. This was enabled by a side-illumined clear plotting screen above the main display, and the use of a white chinagraph pencil and small ruler to construct the necessary vectors. Today's navigators can benefit from upright daylight screens with processed data and computer-aided plots and graphics to achieve the same results.

Far ahead, what looked like a traditional centre-castle cargo vessel gradually rose above the horizon. It appeared to be at anchor and evidently close to the charted position of the Practicos light vessel. This is the major aid to navigation for ships making the pilotage station and channel up the River Plate. Other vessels began to appear, then parts of Montevideo itself. Preconditioned as to how a light vessel looks by the many elegant red-hulled examples purpose-built by London's Corporation of Trinity House, it dawned that the large ship ahead was indeed the Practicos. Black hulled with buff superstructure and cargo derricks, its main optic appeared disproportionally small, sited atop the foremast. Eventually, at a range of only 2 miles, the word PRACTICOS could be discerned on the vessel's side.

As part of the pre-arrival preparations, *John Biscoe*'s ensign of the Falkland Islands had been hoisted. Later, the Uruguay national flag had been raised as a traditional courtesy, in the respectful priority location at the forward-most halyard on the starboard side. The ship was slowed to make good her required time of arrival at the approach buoy to the channel to Montevideo. The substantial pilot launch *Ederra* delivered the pilot. Although pilotage here is compulsory, Capt. Elliott was well acquainted with the port and steered the ship in personally. As an advisor, the pilot was happy to assume the role of informed bystander, offering answers to occasional queries.

Assured of a berth alongside Darsena II dock, *John Biscoe* passed smoothly into the extensive harbour. At the dock, a fleet of ocean-going fishing vessels was sandwiched together, their sterns to the quay. Room at the berth was very snug, presenting a small challenge to get alongside and moored. The timed entry into the Deck Log: RFWE – rung finished with engines – was a satisfying close to that particular voyage. The ship's company had three full days ahead to combine dusting off long-stowed shoreside clothing with routine work in port. Yet for some but newly joined, it was an unexpected and less than fully earned bonus!

The ship's gangway was no sooner rigged than all the port officials and their followers came aboard, inundating the wardroom and infusing it with an exotic physical presence of Latin America. Suitably potent drinks were the anticipated lubricant to oil the processes of port entry. Soon afterwards the wives of crew members who had been waiting patiently on the quay were able to board, to be welcomed and proudly introduced.

To the crew who had been away for months and who had seen perpetual work for half of the season, tying up at the fringe of a bustling city brought prospects to stir their energies. Those who had been aboard for only a few days felt spoilt, not only at having such an early break, but also at being on the doorstep of Uruguay's captivating capital.

Outward travel from England, and the immediate immersion into the seagoing shift pattern of watch-keeping for a ship on passage, had given the body clock some exercise in adjustment. Plunged once again into a day-work situation in port, with the potential for uninterrupted night-time sleep, the system was again thrown into confusion, but one which is part and parcel of shipboard life. With temperatures back in the mid-twenties, I had experienced several climate changes in quick succession. Without air conditioning on the ship, my cabin fans had whirred incessantly.

Slumbering on the open boat deck beneath their tarpaulins, the three inflatable Humber workboats had also suffered from the daytime

John Biscoe at Montevideo, Uruguay, for mid-season 'Rest and Recuperation'. (Author's collection)

brightness and heat. They had become drum tight from the attentions of direct sun and the lack of cooling breeze. Like sighs of evident relief, the excess pressure had been released through the valves. Robustly made, these boats had seen much testing service in the transfer of people, equipment and goods between ship and the permanent Antarctic bases and temporary field stations. Through time and experience, little additions had been made. Their maintenance and use in a variety of operations was to become a regular feature for me, and a chance for skilled colleagues to train me in turn, to become fit for purpose. In the after fan-room adjacent, I was introduced to the well-provided workshop, dedicated to these boats. Some 35-hp Mercury outboards were cradled on a stand; a workbench was served by drawers and racks of comprehensive spares; mysterious-looking earmuffs turned out to be devices to deliver fresh cooling water to the engines so that they could be run and flushed out, before and after use.

Sunday at Montevideo: the dock environs were as quiet as the near-deserted ship. In company with the duty engineer, it was not an arduous task to be Day Duty Deck Officer. Those of the crew who lived locally wished to have time ashore. Second officer John was one such, understandably hoping to spend as much time as possible with his wife, a native of the city. Offering cover aboard ship is a seafaring tradition between colleagues, and the favour will be returned on later occasions.

Pinning a card on my cabin door, indicating my status as duty officer, I merely had to keep myself on call and carry out regular rounds. Covering the twelve-hour period from 8 p.m., a continuous deck watch was maintained by one of the crew, acting as night-watchman, under the guidance of written orders posted on the bridge. On its page it extolled appropriate requirements: tend gangway and moorings as required; ensure gangway is properly lit; carry out hourly fire patrols, otherwise continuous deck watch. Flags up and lights off at sunrise. No unauthorised persons allowed onboard. Call Night Duty Officer if required. Morning calls: cooks and stewards as normal, unless by other arrangement; Night Duty Officer at 0730.

The call came before then. The shore waterman had arrived early, to begin replenishing the ship's fresh water. From the little forklift, the hose reels were run out, brought aboard over the low well deck and unkinked into smooth curves to avoid blockage. The end was passed back over the side to be flushed through with the first of the water, before directing it into the ship's open filling pipe. The snug-fitting wooden plug was removed from the tank ventilator. A gentle stream of displaced air emerged to caress an enquiring hand, confirming that the tank was filling.

Hovering in the passageway outside the pantry, early-bird salesmen from local firms stood and chattered, dispensing promotional leaflets. Leather factories seemed common. I ordered a custom-made wallet, supplying a full-size pattern taken from the ancient and decaying specimen that had served for many years. Due for return to Montevideo in March, I awaited the outcome with patient interest: I would have little direct need for a wallet or its contents in the intervening months.

Visits to the city required a pass in order to successfully run the gauntlet of the petty powers in uniforms which may inhabit dock gatehouses. Discreet holes in boundary fences are of traditional benefit to seafarers the world over, often considerably reducing distance and avoiding occasional confrontation with officialdom.

To many taking a run ashore, the availability of local currency on a ship is taken almost for granted. Providing this facility is just one of the many routine tasks of any ship's agent. On a daily basis a goodly supply was delivered to the ship's master, then on to the issuing officer, to be given out as a 'shore sub' upon request. 'When are you giving out the subs then Third?' was a question often asked in passing. Queuing outside my cabin, each hopeful recipient trooped in to ponder their solvency. £50 translated into 150,000 of the local currency. Wielding the limp and unfamiliar notes took mental agility; big figures represented small sums. Into the record book went the names, the amounts and the many styles of signature, accompanied by the additional exchange of small talk about events ashore, which can act as the local bush telegraph.

Meal times in port are often compromised, a source of general irritation. During lunch the port authorities advised that we would have to 'shift ship' about 100 feet astern to allow quay space for yet another large fishing vessel. Achieving such an apparently simple end requires an inordinate amount of organising, and effort by many hands. Rat guards from the moorings were removed; ropes were taken in or transferred along the quay to different bollards; the gangway netting was freed; the gangway itself was craned aboard, the captain himself at the controls. Railings were replaced to close the yawning gap; portable radios were harnessed to keep in touch with the parties at bow, stern and on the bridge. The language barrier with shore linesmen made certain communication difficult; problems ashore with ropes are best sorted out by the ship's crew. In his orange boiler suit, the captain went ashore to do just that. Everybody available was called.

Finally prepared, and with appropriate ropes led onto the winches at each end, the ship was gradually hauled astern. Easing out on other ropes which would finally halt the ship's motion, the off-going Captain Phelps enjoyed playing a hands-on role, perhaps with a hint of nostalgia to counter his impending retirement. His professional connection with *John Biscoe* spanned the previous twenty-five years. Banter between him and

All ranks muster to 'shift ship'; quay space in Montevideo was at a premium. (Author's collection)

Captain Elliott was founded on a long-shared history. Only they could fully appreciate the tease 'whoever was on that rope – sack him!' Given the universal sign of crossed forearms to indicate 'make fast', with the ship at her new position the check-ropes were made up quickly on to the bitts. Additional ropes were again sent out and secured, likewise the rat guards and gangway. An hour had passed. Lunches were retrieved from the pantry hot press and consumed elsewhere than the wardroom, to avoid the delay and effort of changing back into uniform.

Early afternoon brought the discovery of a shady pursuit during the previous night. The ship's video recorder had vanished from its cabinet in the wardroom. The incident left a nasty aftertaste and a sense of suspicion towards the shore watchmen who attended the vessel and who, for the most part, appeared to laze inattentive in cosy corners, essentially immune to the polite suggestions of the ship's staff.

Some new faces appeared on the ship. In reality they were old hands, as cordial greetings were exchanged with familiar colleagues who were to take over from those about to go on leave. Formal handovers were mixed with reminiscences and the latest gossip, little groups gathering in cabins as yet more drinks were gratefully accepted. In the bags of those returning to Britain was mail from those staying aboard throughout Christmas and well beyond. It was a more certain and rapid courier than by local means.

From mid-afternoon a lowering sky brought a sultry heaviness which found release in thunder. A steady rain was occasionally bolstered by heavier downpours. Intent on using our limited free time for an evening ashore, in company with Hamish, the catering officer, we could only cock our eyes skywards and don waterproofs. We found the hole in the fence and plunged headlong into the dark unknown of the city.

Beyond the docks lay broken slums and squalor, old litter clogging gutters and decorating the haphazard pavements. As the rain bounced and steamed from the ground it was accompanied by a subtly nauseous scent. Sheltering ourselves in doorways further up the incline, we watched fascinated as the torrent of run-off swept by in broad swathes. Passing vehicles threw up a forging wake of spray and lunged drunkenly into unseen potholes. There were few walking the streets. Umbrellas were evident; some had surrendered to a drenched fate. One boy had given up the struggle and ran with bare torso, his clothes in a plastic bag.

At the Plaza Independencia a huge statue of a national hero on horseback, elevated high on a towering plinth, pointed down the length of the main street. The roads were laid out in a regular pattern and criss-crossed at right angles. Even this main thoroughfare was little occupied, as trolleybuses and their more ordinary counterparts cruised by in toilsome anonymity. Hamish and I succumbed to the light and promise of life from the Manchester Bar, a corner café with an unexpectedly British name. It enabled us to quit our soaking anoraks and take to a welcome booth.

Despite his seven previous years away from the sea, my companion seemed to converse confidently with the homely and smiling waiter. Through occasional gesticulations and verbal experiments our order was made: white coffees and a small glass of water each. There soon followed an abundance of fare, served up under the title Preparacion Especial, a *carte blanche* order which seemed to give free rein to the creativity of the cooks. A myriad of small dishes was spread across the table, each with different delicacies, hot and cold. Later, a second tray was brought, completely filling the tabletop. Thus a local custom was tried, as others sat round about in companionable groups, having an evening away from their own normalities. Farewells were eventually exchanged with the waiter in a hand clasp of *bonhomie*, transcending the barrier of language and nationality.

If the name of Manchester Bar had echoed from our homeland, so too had the familiar logo and corporate livery of two Shell road tankers, which sat on the quay as close as practicable to the *John Biscoe*. Delivering fuel, the heavy umbilical hose spanned the well deck and was connected to the inlet manifold. Bunkering is a waiting and monitoring operation, so the ship's engineers stood watch on deck nearby. On the foremast halyard the red 'B' flag fluttered, indicating to a wider audience that dangerous goods were being transferred. At the same time, towards the stern, food stores in a cargo net were being hoisted aboard by the ship's crane. In white boiler suits, the catering staff emerged on to the after deck to hump the heavy bags of potatoes and boxes of vegetables into the lift, for transfer and storage below decks in the dedicated compartments. Bunkers completed, the tankers departed, to be replaced soon afterwards by a smaller tanker. It was empty, ready to receive 5 tonnes of oily waste sludge from the ship.

Scientists from BAS destined for bases in the Antarctic had begun to arrive. Known by tradition as FIDs, from the days when the organisation was called the Falkland Islands Dependencies Survey, the name had lingered with affection. The principal scientist was referred to as the King Fid. Their absorption aboard took place without fuss, as they had their own deck and facilities.

The time of sailing was set for ten o'clock on the morning of 19 December. Requesting a call from the watchman at seven o'clock provided an early start, for pre-sailing preparations. The ship and the day were still in repose. It was pleasant for a leisurely wake-up to sup tea over the rail before rounds on deck. Stepping ashore briefly for the last time, armed with pen and paper, the draught marks at bow and stern were read and noted: 13 feet 7 inches forward; 18 feet 1 inch aft. Back aboard, the mean draught was calculated to enable these and other related measurements to be entered on the Draught Sheet, for endorsing by the master. An official document, it is required to be posted in a conspicuous place prior to a ship sailing. The draught is also requested by port officials.

Preparing any vessel for sea involves all departments. On the bridge, equipment hummed into life: gyro compass repeater headings were aligned with the gyro itself; bearing mirrors were replaced on their bridge-wing pedestals; comparisons were made with the magnetic compass; VHF radios were tuned to appropriate channels; charts and navigational equipment were made ready. With a careful scan around the harbour in case of shipping movements, the whistle was tested. In the steering-gear compartment, an engineer inspected the operation of the steering motors, in the modes selected and operated on the bridge, in voice contact throughout.

The ship's agent made his final visit, as did Customs and Immigration. Off-going personnel made their own final rounds and farewells. With another day in Montevideo before their flights home, they took up station on the quayside as spectators, to salute the ship on her latest journey into the South.

At the breakfast table, the next round of new faces appeared, including the senior FID who traditionally ate in the wardroom. Enthusiastic talk was exchanged; the prospect of discovering the remainder of 'Jimmy Rossaurus'

Taking on stores and fuel bunkers at Montevideo. (Author's collection)

Safe in port, radio officer Maurice O'Donnell attends a faulty radar scanner. (Author's collection)

– the fossilised dinosaur found on James Ross Island – provided for novel conversation.

Clear of the berth and with all ropes reported as inboard, the ship moved slowly ahead. Seeking assurance from the pilot that there was no problem in using the whistle, farewell blasts from its strident two-tone discord thundered about the harbour. In answer, the diminishing figures on the quayside waved. Each would feel inner tuggings as the ship left their sight. Perhaps none more so than Captain Phelps, associated with her for so many years, not only as Master but also as her superintendent during the yearly refits in Britain. Little did he know then that his own fitting and final 'send off' was only months away, and that it would be forever linked with that of *John Biscoe*.

Tied up alongside larger and sombre-hued naval vessels in the outer harbour, bright in her red hull and two funnels, *Pedro Campbell* looked small but distinguished. The support ship for Uruguay's presence in Antarctica, she appeared as a mirror to *John Biscoe*, in her understated yet enduring strength. Suddenly the bridge VHF radio pronounced, '*John Biscoe, John Biscoe*, this is the British merchant ship, *Churchill*.' The English voice and its message came as an unexpected and pleasant surprise, as eyes were cast around the harbour in search of this patriotic vessel. She was easily located, discharging containers at a commercial berth. As *John Biscoe* passed her, revealing her red ensign at the stern, cordial greetings for Christmas were exchanged, with wishes for a safe passage into the Antarctic.

Our departure from harbour was sedate, constrained by the careful movements of a large elderly tanker in ballast. Partially out of the water, her huge propeller thrashed beneath her copious stern. The wide channel ran north–south, marked laterally by red and green buoys, in opposite fashion to that found in Europe. In the Americas and certain other areas of the world, 'System B' buoyage is used where the channel marks are interpreted when leaving a port. The more widely adopted 'System A' views channels and their buoyage when entering port. As always, international agreements need compromises, and care in avoiding confusion.

The pilot having disembarked, an initial southerly course was set. In the first hour, Montevideo slipped below the horizon but remained in the form of a still-helpful radar echo, which, coupled with the isolated target of the light vessel, allowed for a reliable course adjustment to counter the east-setting outfall current from the River Plate. At noon, the ship passed the final radio reporting point for Montevideo Control. Signing off and returning to the listening watch on Channel 16, *John Biscoe* was a free-roaming creature of the ocean once more.

The ship's complement having been swelled by the newly joined FIDs, a safety talk and boat muster were organised for the traditional time of 16.15. Prominently posted about the vessel, the muster lists detailed the various signals, duties and actions for emergency, man overboard and abandon ship situations. As the continuous sounding of the whistle and alarm bells announced the muster, the ship's company took up station on the boat deck. All suitably clad in appropriate clothing, the newcomers were apprised of the three lifeboats and two davit-launched life rafts. Large deck lockers were opened for the issue and donning of life jackets. A tally of names was made at each station, instruction was then given, voices competing with the outdoor sounds of engine noise and fans. The advice about seasickness and hypothermia amused some listeners, sensitive for the moment to its seeming incongruity with the calm and warmth of the day, which lingered into the evening.

Never one to miss an opportunity, the bosun took advantage of the weather to engage his crew in maintenance of the cargo-handling equipment, preparing for both forthcoming use and protection from the weather. The cargo wires for the derricks were removed from their drums then heavily greased as they were slowly fed back on, a metal scraper serving to tap each turn tightly against its neighbour. The next day also provided ideal conditions to continue the work. The foremast not only provided a structure for the elevated crow's nest and searchlight, and its role in carrying navigation lights and connections for radio aerials, but was a king post to support the operation of the two cargo derricks. As such its wire stays were substantial.

The task assigned to senior crewman Martin was to 'black down the stays' – to coat them with a protective compound concocted from a sticky mix of Stockholm tar and varnish. Supported by several of his colleagues, Martin was to be monkey man. Scaling the mast to its very truck with a light line, a heavier rope and pulley block were hauled aloft and secured, to support a bosun's chair. Kitted out with an old boiler suit, safety harness and a Blackpool promenade head-protection of cloths secured with string, Martin was hauled aloft unceremoniously. A bucket of tar accompanied him. The hoisting rope was cast around a bulwark cleat and eased out to lower him gradually down the incline of the stays. Copiously covering each stay on his descent, feet clasped around the wire beneath, any stray drops which fell to the deck were quickly mopped up. Thankful for a lack of headwind, the white expanse of the bridge-front was spared a spattering.

Preparations of a more genteel nature were underway in the wardroom as steward Shaun put up the Christmas decorations. In the electrician's cabin, an artistic conspiracy was being hatched for the souvenir edition of the Christmas Day menu.

The weekly emergency drill was again due, held in the afternoon at the start of the 4 p.m. watch period; but what would it be? The signals would be sounded, but which signals? Different responses would be required. Three long blasts on the whistle confirmed a suspicion: it was a man-overboard drill. As junior off-watch officer my station was as coxswain of the standby rescue boat. Required to be dressed in an immersion suit, which was always hung up in readiness behind the cabin door, the seconds it took to put on felt like minutes. Overhead, others of the crew made ready the two Humber boats: covers off; engines mounted and briefly started; the crane swung into action. Throughout, the ship was tightly manoeuvring. Instigator of the drill, the captain turned *John Biscoe* short round, keen to get the casualty ahead as soon as possible. Lookouts were directed to maintain visual sighting. A timekeeper recorded progress. In four minutes the boat and crew were ready to launch. In thirteen minutes the casualty, in the form of a plastic barrel, had been recovered aboard. Afterwards a debriefing on the bridge evaluated the exercise. A report would later appear on the notice boards, for the benefit of all.

As the dummy casualty was being recovered, a further exercise was broadcast. The ship's steering gear had failed, requiring the emergency steering arrangements to be operated. Accompanying the engineers into the steering flat, the locally controlled mechanisms were engaged, as communications to the bridge were established. Beneath our feet reverberated the muffled thrashing of the propeller. A variety of helm orders was received: port 10°; starboard 15°; midships; steer 150°. A gyro compass repeater clicked mechanically as the ship swung, the rudder turned by the replica wheel adjacent. It was an odd sensation on a non-naval vessel, to steer without any visual reference to the outside world.

The trio of tests to the ship's systems, and the crew's familiarity with them, concluded with a session with the emergency fire pump. Traditionally placed away from the main machinery space, on *John Biscoe* it was located in the bow-thrust compartment, well forward and near to the keel. Led once more by the engineers, the Lister engine nestled cosily under its hessian cover. Nearby, instructions were posted, detailing its operation: sea suction and outlet valves open; a hydrant open on deck; oil levels checked; throttle set; decompression lever open; hand-crank located – held properly to avoid breaking the thumb; turn the engine over, build up speed; flick two levers closed and quickly pull out the handle as the engine fires. To those newly initiated it was a source of relief to achieve the task without physical injury or wounded pride in being unable to crank fast enough. Satisfaction came with the engine's healthy roar and a thumbs-up gesture from the grinning engineer.

It was 21 December. In the northern hemisphere there would be impending celebrations and the marking of the winter solstice, the longest night of the year. In the southern, it was midsummer, with weather to match. In the ship's Nautical Almanac, giving daily tabulated astronomical details, the sun's declination for this day bore testimony to its southernmost limit, lingering for hours above the Tropic of Capricorn at 23°, 26½ minutes south, before its inexorable movement northwards. To the pessimistic mariner this gave the opportunity to wax grimly that the nights would be starting to draw in again.

It was a fine day for varnish work. The sliding bridge doors and stout wooden taff rails bordering the bridge-wings were the captain's pride and joy. Over the years he had lavished personal attention on their appearance, building up a smooth and glossy finish. Of late, the rails had suffered from the scuffing of rope, used to regularly draw surface water samples in a special little rubber bucket, to obtain its temperature. With a light-hearted admonition he scolded the watch-keepers for allowing this malpractice from the lookouts. Having selected a suitable grade of wet-and-dry paper, with a pail of water close by and attired in his orange boiler suit, Captain Elliot's latest tribute to traditional bright work saw his annual project carefully rubbed down and cleaned. By evening the wings were roped off from deck access, as the drying woodwork gleamed anew. At the midnight hour, the image of the westering crescent moon reflected faultlessly from the handrails.

* * *

The Magellan Field Sat Nav set was an unassuming little box, the size of a transistor radio. Held in the King Fid's hand, the geographical position it registered was comparable with the ship's fixed installation. Clearly, for those days, it was an impressive piece of equipment, offering an assurance of position finding during the anticipated weeks of isolation to come on James Ross Island, near the tip of the Antarctic Peninsula.

Payslips for December were hardly expected, yet the chief officer was distributing them during the morning. With head office in Cambridge closing for the holiday period, their surprise arrival provoked close scrutiny. Perhaps the benign offer of money in the bank early was for Christmas shopping by far-off relatives. The slips became a conversation point for comparison and comment, a reason for mutterings about tax and the excesses of shipboard bar bills and subs for visits ashore.

Handing over the watch after midnight to second officer John, the ship was some 30 miles to the east of the Falklands. There was quiet conjecture about how the weather would be when crossing the Drake Passage, that notorious stretch of ocean that lies wholly exposed to the excesses of the westerlies that rotate about the southern continent. So far that season, whenever *John Biscoe* had crossed either north- or southwards it was rough, defying comfort and sleep by inducing heavy rolling from a beam sea that was impracticable to counter.

By early breakfast the wind and sea conditions had indeed become fresh, the ship lurching in response. In the wardroom Shaun was running late because of the motion. The vacuum cleaner was still being directed beneath the tables, as the cornflakes slopped about the plate. The non-slip table coverings held the place settings firm, but an occasional napkin broke free while the marmalade jar rocked irritatingly on its ill-matched saucer. The curtains and Christmas decorations swayed in unison to the heady rhythm beneath the ship.

South of the Falklands lies an extensive area of comparative shallows. A broad plateau called the Burdwood Bank, it is some 200 miles wide, rising from the surrounding depths to 60 metres in places. On the bridge navigation table was spread a chart entitled Drake Passage. Its recorded features evoked awe and respect. Towards the top lay the Falkland Islands, the tip of South America, Tierra del Fuego, the Strait of Magellan and Cape Horn. The South Shetland Islands were to be found depicted at the bottom. The gap in-between represented several hundred miles of unremitting ocean, across which a bold pencil line was drawn: our prospective track. At the present, between the Falklands and Burdwood Bank, it seemed the conditions were a prelude to yet another uncomfortable crossing. Thankfully, on this occasion, we were to be proved wrong.

Leaning on the chart table, in reminiscent mood, chief officer Robin chatted with Mike, the King Fid. Pencil in hand, he meandered across the chart, describing previous voyages: an unusual run through the Chilean islands on the larger BAS icebreaker *Bransfield*, their location off Tierra del Fuego at the onset of the Falklands conflict, and of their timely run south, marred for several hours by mechanical breakdown.

Blue sky prevailed, to enliven the sea's turmoil, highlighting the breaking waves, casting rainbows across the deck from the spindrift. Delighting in their mastery of the elements, the accompanying birds performed, each to their own habit: flitting pale grey prions; the quiet-natured cape pigeons; black-browed albatrosses, perpetually frowning as if registering a permanent nautical disapproval; the huge and majestic wandering albatrosses, with their pink beaks and benign expression. Occasional mats of drifting kelp weed showed as warm patches of olive.

By evening, with the echo sounder running, the approach to Burdwood Bank was marked graphically by the rotating pen trace, the burnt thin black line climbing up through the ranges, before its eventual plunge to several thousand metres. Thus *John Biscoe* once more began to traverse the Drake Passage. The eventual march of distance and time was marked by the succession of positions on the chart, the waxing moon, the lengthening twilights, and the increasing altitude of the stellar pattern of the Southern Cross.

The sea uncharacteristically continued to moderate overnight, and the wind to veer on to the quarter. Christmas Eve morning dawned with a pearly overcast of uniform grey, yet, with a startling and unnatural brightness, a pair of birds in flight captivated the eye. Based on the information in the bridge reference book *Birds of the Antarctic and Sub Antarctic* they appeared to be American sheathbills. Disliked by the chief officer, in numbers they were apparently attracted to the orange boat-covers, where they felt compelled to leave their unwelcome calling cards.

By mid-watch the charted position showed that the ship had crossed a wavy dotted line, labelled the Antarctic Convergence. On page one of the Admiralty's *Antarctic Sailing Directions*, an explanation was offered:

> The Southern Ocean is divided into two main hydrological zones by the Antarctic Convergence. This is the line along which the cold north-going Antarctic surface water sinks beneath the warmer sub-Antarctic water. In many places it can be distinguished by the sudden change in surface temperature, and is fairly constant in position. The two zones influence distribution of marine life and the properties of the overlying air-masses.

Crossing this singular boundary was an event of some moment. Accompanied by an atmospheric murk and steady rain, it was a signpost and harbinger of the ice realm that was drawing ever closer beyond the southern horizon.

It was evidently an age-old argument, raised each year by the FIDs prior to them embarking on their isolated field expeditions. Armed with compasses as part of their standard equipment, suddenly the properties of the Earth's magnetic field assumed significance. Seeking reassurance from the bridge, the invariable question was, 'Do you add or subtract East Variation from a magnetic bearing to make it a true bearing?' By rote, and temporarily forgetting mathematical principles, the navigator can fall back on the common maxim: 'Compass to True; East is Right … so add!' The perplexed scientists were sceptical. It fell to Simon, the multitalented chief engineer, to diplomatically provide a satisfyingly graphic and scientific solution.

Such bizarre requests were not unusual. Later on in the watch the medical doctor asked if the ship's motion could be made any steadier, as he needed to take an X-ray of a crew member's foot which had been causing problems. The one-second exposure would be compromised by movement and engine vibration. When all had been prepared, the ship was hove-to. The manoeuvre had been the first real opportunity for me to start acquiring the 'feel' of controlling the ship, so useful and necessary in her sphere of routine operations – medical or otherwise.

Instilled with the need to adopt a whole new ethos of navigational caution, from noon onwards bridge lookouts were doubled, alternating hour-about, to enhance concentration. During the evening, the air and sea temperatures hovered close to zero. The crisp air made the cheeks glow and tingle. There was muted excitement at the possibility of encountering first ice. The shadow of every breaking wave ahead was subjected to careful scrutiny, as if a place of ambush for rogue growlers of rock-hard and translucent lumps of ice. Instead, a solitary penguin acknowledged our presence before it withdrew in short porpoising leaps: we had been welcomed at the door of Antarctica.

CHAPTER 2

An Alien and Extraordinary Beauty

Christmas at the South Shetland Islands – Skirmishes with ice – Signy base – New Year at Hope Bay.

It was to be a Christmas Day like no other.

The chief officer described the morning weather as 'South Shetland mank'. A thin, dank fog prevailed. On handing over the watch he advised that he had recorded in the log the detection of a single SRT – a stationary radar target – taking it to have been an iceberg. Half an hour later I received a dubious gift of my own on this Christmas morning. As the atmospheric veil grew thicker, I too detected a faint stationary target on the radar screen. It seemed more than coincidence that the echo lay exactly beneath the obscuring line that represented the ship's head – our direction of travel. It felt like walking towards a quietly intimidating bouncer at the door of a very frigid club. This SRT of my own also appeared solitary and was to be my first ever encounter with such ice. Destined never to set eyes on it I took the prescribed open-water action of avoidance, passing it to windward with a clearance of 2 miles.

In bold and confident numbers, fathom depths were shown on the chart. Delicately drawn additions in magenta ink pointed to later information, usually of spot depths far less than those generally denoted. The invaluable *Antarctic Pilot* book advises of these hazards, called *vigias*, as dangerous shoals rising precipitously from deep water. The ship's recorder had been indicating a continual reduction in depth, the range scales being changed to keep pace with the trace. The line seemed relentless in its pursuit of reaching the surface.

Having previously mentioned this anomalous trend, it drew interest in other quarters, and a respect for what the recorder seemed to be showing. In prudence, and with the captain properly informed, speed was quickly reduced. Beneath its canvas cover in the bridge corner, the sonar was brought into rapid use. On its angled screen a bright green image was painted, another graphic form of gauging distance, using a different source of sound. A quiet ping emanated from a small loudspeaker to accompany the moving green dot sent out across the sonar screen. Beneath the water, as the probing pulse of sound hit a reflecting surface, a corresponding croak assailed the ears, as a broad bubble shape appeared on the screen. It indicated that not 80 fathoms lay beneath the keel, but the anticipated 800. The sea's teasing had been identified as a thermocline, a boundary between water masses with differing densities. How often had mariners' equipment been essentially confused? Could recorded shoal depths have been figments of this fluctuating thermocline? With *John Biscoe*'s newly acquired data stored, an official Hydrographic Note was compiled for eventual dispatch to the Admiralty. By such small and painstaking contributions the veracity of navigational knowledge is advanced, in a region where much is far from comprehensive.

In cabins throughout the ship, at varying times the carefully stored Christmas gifts were removed from drawers and cases. Wrapped and presented early at home, they were to greatly enhance the day, and mark it out as a truly special occasion. Cards and small decorations enlivened cabins as, for a while, their occupants were transported by such things to people and places far away. The chief officer was happy: he had forgotten to pack his watercolours. No doubt spotted at home, the plump tubes of Winsor & Newton colours and paper clearly made his day. A tiny red-and-gold Christmas tree adorned my desk, a gift from a lady with whom I had then been out on only one date. Thankfully she didn't take it personally that I had promptly disappeared to the furthest outpost of the planet for half a year, although at that stage neither of us foresaw marriage over another distant horizon.

By mid-afternoon the ship had rounded the eastern end of King George Island, in the South Shetlands group. Beneath a heavy but bright and snow-laden sky, *John Biscoe* approached the location of her Christmas anchorage, in King George Bay on the island's south coast. Clad against the chill and the snow flurries, eager observers took to the open decks. Entry was pre-planned, with references and clearing lines drawn on the chart. The ship made her measured approach. A solitary islet, known as Martello Tower, looking like a Southern Ocean Rockall, was used as a transit with a distinguishable mountain summit. Swinging on to a course which pointed

Splendid isolation for Christmas, in the South Shetland Islands. (Author's collection)

towards the low humped form of Growler Rock, the desired anchorage position lay close ahead, at the margins of the bay.

At the bow, the bosun's mate and second officer stood by, the port anchor having been cleared and lowered to the water, ready for letting go. Making slight sternway, the order was given. With a thunderous clanking, and eyes averted from the haze of metallic dust, the cable rattled out of its locker. As the length marks came successively into view, the bell was rung accordingly, reinforced by gloved fingers raised towards the bridge. With six shackles of chain run out, equal to 90 fathoms' length, the ship brought up quietly to her tether. The warning black anchor ball was hoisted at the forestay, for the needs of professional etiquette rather than necessity. The engines having come to rest, an underlying stillness enveloped the ship. Appreciative eyes scanned the dramatic surroundings of the sheltered waters that had welcomed us so benignly.

The snow clouds lifted, the air cleared, and the full glorious aspect of King George Bay was revealed. On the horizon sat the first iceberg to be properly seen, grounded between Penguin Island and the main shore. A huge regular block, it emanated an otherworldly blue glow. Pristine smooth white expanses of ice cap ended in blue-tinted cliffs, sculpted into weathered and

At anchor, the ship's main engines and control room are stilled. (Author's collection)

contorted patterns, worried by the sea at their base. Mountainous crags reared up in the distance. High up on the bare slopes of the prominent and angular islet of Lion's Rump, a large colony of penguins resided, stirring curiosity about their ungainly endeavours to reach such heights. A lone stony beach offered potential for landing, beneath arid-seeming slopes only partially covered by snow. Slight movements in the shallows, and dark smudges reposing on the ice, betrayed the presence of seals.

The anchor watch routine was adopted: one seaman lookout on bridge-watch; an officer on call. Given the luxury of not needing to relieve the bridge watchkeeper for evening meal, there was time to pay visits and share in the Christmas cheer. I was urged into the cabin of George, the bosun's mate, who expansively filled and presented a tumbler of rum. A tough and spritely fifty, and a shipmate of good cheer, our worlds quickly grew small as we discovered we had lived in houses within yards of each other. We concurred that our local North Shields chip shop used to make excellent fish suppers.

Ritually attired in formal dress uniform, the dinner table was graced by Sue, one of the outdoor survival experts who would so ably support their scientific charges in the months to come. It was a rare chance for her to dress up in a style less masculine than that which is usually demanded by necessity on the ship, a genteel contrast to the expected realities of working in a field party on James Ross Island. In only a few days, several groups were scheduled to be landed. Little could be known then of the dramatic events that would befall such plans, events that are part of the normality of being subject to the unconquerable whims of the Antarctic.

Light in plenty prevailed at midnight. More as a festive token, the ship's deck lights were switched on. They added visual warmth, enlivening the pillar-box red of mast and derricks, and the weathered green of the hatch tarpaulins. On the broad and pale face of the bridge front, the rectangular windows of the wardroom each mutely spoke of homeliness amid the embracing vastness of our isolation.

Given that the previous day had been dominated by the usual needs of work, Boxing Day was officially decreed to be our own particular Christmas, and came complete with all the trimmings. Despite its desolation, the shore beckoned, simply because it was the local terra firma, a venue other than the ship to stretch the legs and, perversely, a viewpoint to look back at our home and regard ourselves in our chosen working environment. 'Shore jollies' were eagerly anticipated. There was no shortage of festive hands to make the workboats ready. The shuttle service was made exhilarating as the boats sped for shore. On an exclusive run I was joined by the captain, who wished to do a spot of surveying in a promisingly sheltered location, for a potential future yacht mooring. Depths were gauged with a leadline, though our recall of the coloured bunting marks was less than perfect.

Afterwards I was given a masterclass in small boat handling, with a demonstration of a particular technique to turn the inflatable deftly round safely through following seas using a trailing anchor, to lie in the shallows bow-on to the weather, and with the outboard engine raised clear of the water, all in one coordinated movement. Hauling hand over hand on the anchor rope allowed the boat to be pulled out through the waves before lowering the engine in deeper water. I learned something new on each practice run until I became reasonably versed in the principle, and was impressed by its effectiveness, which was eventually to stand me in good stead. Meanwhile, in the other boat, John had ventured into more precipitous parts, to obtain a lump of glacier ice for eventual use in the celebratory drinks.

The first shore parties were refreshed by their morning constitutional along the strand, which was littered with numerous pieces of bleached whale backbone. Immature elephant seals lay, mainly in recumbent heaps, occasionally flipping sand over their backs, or raising a reluctant eyelid to inspect the strange visitors. Sounds of flatulence were not infrequent and their breath was uncomplimentary. In the shallows two young bulls engaged in mock battle, up-rearing and hurling themselves into heavy, blubber-rippling blows.

In the wardroom there were drinks for the officers and FIDs at eleven o'clock. The crew and FIDs took their lunch towards midday. The catering department had risen to the challenge of making the Christmas celebration special, with a sumptuous meal to remember. Only later on could they themselves surrender to the delayed gratification of their own meal-taking. The wardroom diners assembled at the table at one o'clock, careful to ensure that silly Christmas-cracker hats were donned at jaunty angles, in good-natured defiance against the black and gold of uniforms. Glasses were charged and Captain Elliott made three toasts: to the Queen; to family and absent friends; and to all who had previously sailed on *John Biscoe*. Other toasts followed: rightly to the cooks and stewards; and generously to Alan the electrician, and to me, whose graphic 'artistry' in menu-making would leave an enduring souvenir of the ship's very last southern Christmas.

Filled with seasonal cheer, the afternoon runs ashore were made before the boats were finally recovered, their engines flushed through and stowed, and the fuel tanks replenished. In the final leisure of evening, a cold buffet and yule log were proffered, for those with any gastronomic gaps left to fill.

At 8 p.m. the ship hummed again with her own life, as the anchor was weighed. Setting a southerly heading across the broad Bransfield Strait towards the Antarctic Peninsula, King George Island slipped from view. In the cool mellowing light, as if from a textbook for beginners in ice navigation, the occasional example was presented to this particular navigator. A single small iceberg came and went in the middle distance. On its slopes, a peppering of tiny dark spots revealed the presence of penguins, and gave an unsettling sense of scale. Next came a jagged and angular bergy bit, still a substantial monolith for definite avoidance. Closer yet came rogue growlers, of infamous reputation. Thus the graded studies continued, and by midway across the strait the ice frequency had increased, a process that was soon to accelerate rapidly.

In normal collision-avoidance situations with other vessels, their shapes generally materialise slowly out of a murky background in a darker tone. Looking through binoculars towards the bearing of anticipated icebergs, they began to subtly loom out of the greyness as a glowing paleness of hue. Close ahead two such bergs shimmered their daunting presence into a harsh reality. It was time to consider how to avoid them. A glance at the outstretched windsock on the masthead amplified the run of small waves, indicating wind direction. The bergs were spaced sufficiently to pass one on either hand. Moved by currents and winds when afloat, it is an easy-to-make, but false, assumption to consider them stationary. They move by an intent which is not their own.

The first was tabular in form, a vertical-sided chunky slab with flat top. The other was sculptural, shapely and rounded. Accessible from the sea, another colony of resting penguins rode on its back. Passing a mile off, when abeam, a slow-motion performance was staged. There seemed a rush of waves, an emergence of ice previously hidden. The berg was rolling over, away from us, to reveal an underside radiant with a glorious palette of yet more pale blues. Having become unstable, and spurred by whatever catalyst, it adjusted spectacularly to its new buoyancy. It had also ruined the penguins' evening.

Quietly proud of his knowledge and experiences from the first half of the voyage, David the young seaman-lookout shared his observations about ice. I listened intently, smiling inwardly at his diplomacy, and pleased that a fellow Geordie found no barriers up and no pretentions to mar communication. We were both on a learning curve; this was his first ever trip to sea. We both would be seeing many things with the receptive eyes of new experience.

Towards midnight the ice lesson beyond the bridge windows had become too complex. In the dusky half-light there lay a huge grounded berg. The radar showed it to be littered round about by ice of other forms. They began to appear everywhere. It seemed impossible to avoid them; slowing down seemed proper. Easing back on the control lever, the engine pulse died away. Unbeknown, in the engine room, Roger, the fourth engineer, had just handed over the watch to Bob with the assurance that all was well. Barely had he finished utterance when, unheralded, the speed reduction came. The presence of ice had sent a shiver of uncertainty through the ship. Reducing speed was a public event, attuned to the pitch of the engine. Each individual would have had a different reaction.

The radar screen was packed with a myriad of echoes of intimidating targets, like ground forces in defence of the stranded berg. I would have to selectively unlearn some of the prudent habits of my navigational lifetime, habits cultivated to carefully avoid all objects. As such I viewed the ice as if it were a concentration of fishing boats, to be negotiated *en masse*. On arrival on the bridge, Captain Elliott encouragingly acknowledged my action as correct in an open-water situation. Here, at the northern approach to Antarctic Sound, a less compromising policy was required. The ice would suffer, and the ship's strengthened hull would be both nurtured and stretched to full capacity. Knowing what that was, the captain increased speed and returned the heading into the thick of the brash of ice. The thud was subtly perceptible, a slight momentary stammer in the ship's progress, felt in the pit of the stomach, but not heard. A growler grumbled down the side and rolled drunkenly in the wake. To answer their combined intimidation by large and frequent course changes would be to court becoming lost in the wider scheme of things. References for safe navigation are scant. Keeping close to the intended track is a sound practice, to avoid unnecessary complications. Stimulated by events, and the wisdom imparted, it was with an effort that I finally surrendered to the cradling pillow of sleep.

* * *

I felt totally overawed, as if literally on another planet; for so it seemed. Woken early by jarring shudders, frequent changes of engine pitch and occasional unnatural heavings, I approached the cabin curtains with a mixed sense of excited foreboding. As live theatre captures its audience and pales the written word, no book-learned imagery had prepared me for the impact of the stage-set before me. Arisen from sleep, I gazed through the glass at a harsh and unforgiving scene of alien and extraordinary beauty.

Dressing in many, yet inadequate, layers, I took to the shelter deck to witness our tortuous progress. At once softened and highlighted by fallen snow, the foredeck appeared re-sculpted, the deck an untrodden plain of white. The atmosphere thick and leaden, it obscured the wider world. We were held in the vice grip of an infinitely superior power. It was intimidating in the extreme to a receptive observer, humbled by the weight of its presence: Antarctica.

There were no landmarks for reassurance, no recognisable images to grasp and quell the disquiet. The world was water in all its forms. Amorphous vapour diffused the light, softening shadows and imposing its wan and sombre pallor on the sea which bore the ice that was undisputed king. From her deferential movements, it was clear that *John Biscoe* was exercising due respect, negotiating the labyrinth of ice architecture that hindered our passage. Descriptive names labelled the various forms, in a vain attempt at taming their cold indifference: floes, growlers, brash, bergy bits, icebergs. Within their cluttered and frigid intimacy the little red-hulled ship asserted gentle defiance. Over the years she too had earned the right to be here.

My own rightful and expected place was on her bridge. Part of my disquiet was in shortly filling those expectations, more self-made than real, in this most unfamiliar of environments. Already I could sense the scene and feel the exercising of experience, free at least for a while to be a solitary spectator.

From the low vantage the way seemed completely blocked. To one side a lofty bluff reared skyward, the only sight of land. Yet I knew this to be a narrow defile, the Fridtjof Sound, gateway into the Erebus and Terror Gulf. Here lay our goal, James Ross Island.

The excessive shuddering resonated throughout the ship. The engines were going astern with a purpose, before ceasing in their labour. We lay motionless; the water churned into fizzing eddies by the pull of the propeller. The contorted barrier ahead spoke of a vast and unrelenting wilderness of ice. The Gulf could not be reached. Retreating stern first, as if afraid to avert the gaze from an antagonist, we gained sufficient open water to turn. There were feelings of both defeat and relief. At the warm comfort of the breakfast table, thoughts were harboured of what would happen next. Many hopes saw their demise in that fateful encounter.

As plans are confounded, more are made; defeat turned to advantage. Our new destination was the South Orkney Islands, and Signy. Here lies a permanent British base which also needed our attentions, its place brought forward on the itinerary. Thus, we were leaving the Trinity Peninsula at the tip of Graham Land, but would return.

The atmosphere on the bridge seemed strangely buoyant, perhaps because retracing steps was less stressful than sounding the unknown. Even so, the passage up the broadening Antarctic Sound, to regain open water many miles to the north, was tortuous enough. My education in ice navigation resumed. Nestled in the bridge recess, close to the central picture window, Captain Elliott lingered, one hand on the engine lever. The other rested lightly on the little steering tiller. The ship responded readily to these delicate controls.

Hefty growlers were gently nudged aside. Reluctant to move, they rasped their defiance along the heavy and scarred plating. Flat sheets of floe ice which barred the way received harsher treatment. The crunch seemed to come too late, as if the ice was insubstantial, or the ship had levitated. As the foreshortening lessened, the speed of our approach seemed to increase, the ice disappearing from view beyond the bow. Impact sounded a weighty rending, as the ship lifted her bulk onto the floe. Jarred to this ungainly halt a swift moment of hesitation passed. The floe yielded and cracked, as the bow slumped heavily, driving home its advantage. The split opened slowly, sucking in an inrush of water to fill the expanding void. Nosing ahead, a path was cleared; until the next time. A heavier floe put up more resistance, the bow sliding off sideways in deflection. The ice foot – submerged ledges which protrude proud of the surface edges – can tear bilge keels or be drawn under the stern to threaten the propeller. Before swinging, it is vital to check behind to see that the way is clear.

Ice is the opponent generally in sight, but the lurking danger of the seabed must never be overlooked. Positions were taken frequently, no easy matter with coastlines of ice cliffs, fringed with bergs. The radar picture had to be scrupulously and continually interpreted. Its display was obliterated by a mass of clutter, not from the usual waves, as in the open sea, but from echoes thrown back from countless reflecting ice surfaces. Areas of lesser concentration showed up more darkly, their orange speckling less dense. Areas initially completely black seemed inviting, but they were radar shadows, cast by the bulky faces of bergs, a taunt to the unwary. They show up by what they conceal beyond as much as by their own painted echoes. Slowly, through the afternoon, the ice lessened its concentration.

The chart, of a route-planning scale, showed our destination of the South Orkney Islands hundreds of miles to the north-east. In my ignorance, I would have assumed the usual course, a straight line drawn towards the southernmost islands in the group. No apparent dangers lay along this route. The dog's leg course, firstly towards Clarence Island, then eastwards to Signy, seemed odd, but the reason was well founded: ice, or at least its expectation. The same southerly winds that had blown for days from the Weddell Sea, pushing pack ice north, would have done the same further east. Theirs could not be a certain charted presence, but experience had guided the hand of the navigator who had planned this particular passage. Open water aided our later progress. Pushed to the north by the approaching edge of the pack ice, only the shrouded snowy heights of Clarence Island could be seen in the distance. It held its drama for the return.

Opening the cabin curtains each morning was often a revelation that could not be adequately contained within the bounds of the small window. On this particular morning watch I was to learn a lot more about growlers. Like gnarled stubs of bared teeth, they lurked with reluctant buoyancy, sluggishly lifting and dipping, determined to lie low in ambush. They hid up-sun, in the direction of our passage. Once astern they showed up beautifully, a grin of dazzling white molars, glinting in a blue dark sea. To one side, the line of pack ice showed solid at the horizon, bordered by ill-defined edges. Negotiating this involved a relentless round of quick decisions, a weaving passage, taking growlers as they came and searching ahead for the line of least resistance.

I was being lured, and fought a losing battle. The ship moved in a galaxy of ice. When I found that avoiding tactics incorporated an element of westerly headings, when east was our goal, I thought it time to consult experts. Thanks to the captain I then attempted and achieved – by my standards – small miracles. At least our destination no longer lay astern!

In the radio room, Maurice was in contact with the base at Signy. Plans were being devised. To this far-flung outpost we were a bearer of fuel and supplies. *John Biscoe* was also an exclusive passenger ship. After completing another two years of work, scientist Andy was looking forward to a year at home. It was gratifying to be an envoy of hope. Our arrival was to be an occasion.

It was a busy afternoon for the deck crew, as there was much to prepare. Activity in the well deck was purposeful. Bringing the two derricks to life and rigging them to their working condition was labour-intensive. Elevated skyward and held by the heavy chain and wire topping lift, their ends were guyed taut to prevent swinging, and linked by a purchase of rope known as the schooner guy. An art form of the seaman's craft, the result was a pleasing symmetry of spars, held static by a harmony of rigging. On its robust structure much weight would be borne.

The Inaccessible Islands were the first to appear: shapely, angular and dark, in contrast to the outlying tabular bergs. The fascination of new places draws the eye, not only to their looming prospect but to their flat images on map and chart. Viewers picked out striking names of features: Despair Rocks; Flensing Island; Sunshine Glacier; and Mount Noble. There was time for such scrutiny, with the ship slowed for arrival in the early hours next morning. On the steady deck, scientists kept fit to the swinging rhythms of the skipping rope. An untimely snag turned an ankle, filling a place at the doctor's surgery.

Calls were made at three o'clock next morning. Fighting against the pull of sleep and the mild injustice of slumber interrupted, a small gathering assembled in the pantry. Each to their own, they attended to their reviving snacks: a bowl of cereal, lemon tea and hot toast, thick black coffee. Consumed with relish, small talk with full mouths was overlooked, as were the crumbs that rained on to jumper fronts.

A glimpse through the porthole had brought disappointment; it was simply a steamy grey neutrality of mist that kept anticipation on the simmer. Giving up secrets slowly seemed the way of these islands, a teasing revelation of more intimate exposure, their substance firming gradually as the drapes of distance fell away. There was only one iceberg in Borge Bay. It lay right on our intended track. Such greetings were taken as normal. The coast of Signy was inhospitable and dramatic, hiding its final secret of Factory Cove and the scientific base to the last. The charted headland spoke of huts, bollards, an oil tank and radio masts: the trappings of a precarious civilisation. The pinpoint of bright light on the hilltop was a monumental beacon against the elements.

On the foredeck, the launch was also elevated from its long repose. It was given a harsh awakening as it was lowered into the water. It seemed to shrink at the chill contact, yet headed valiantly shoreward, bearing the mail. It would see much service during the day.

Tiny islets named Small Rock and Bare Rock were the guardian pillars at the entrance to the cove. These slipped by, close on either side. With long familiarity Captain Elliott conned the ship. It was to be an involved and exacting mooring. As the only newcomer, it was to be another wide-eyed education to see the old hands exercise their skills, all in a cauldron of adverse weather. Both anchors were ready, each to be dropped in turn as the captain's hand fell. Edging the ship forward until his judgement whispered 'now', his gesture brought immediate response. Anchoring is always dramatic. The heavy chain clanked out in time with forward progress. Movement checked, the second anchor echoed its fellow. Technical books would describe the manoeuvre as a running moor. It was seamanship that brought an appreciative smile.

Radios were alive with fresh voices and the clipped messages of the operation. From the base, a fast inflatable bore parties to Mooring Point and Billie Rocks. At these unlikely spots, mooring ropes were to be secured; a belt-and-braces approach was needed in this exposed location. Of more pressing need, ropes from the stern were towed ashore and passed to willing hands. Their labours seemed toilsome, slow in the extreme. Aboard, nerves chafed until the ropes could be hauled taut, bringing the swinging stern under control off the unforgiving rocky shore. Sent away from either bow, the inflatable pulled out two head-ropes, like seals' whiskers. A full length and more of rope was used, trailing in a curved floating bight, a

John Biscoe moored off Signy base, South Orkney Islands, for shoreside replenishment operations. Sunshine Glacier in the background. (Author's collection)

Belt-and-braces against severe weather; bow ropes and two anchors keep *John Biscoe* off the rocks astern. (Author's collection)

hindrance to the inflatable already struggling against the deflecting hand of the wind. 'There must be better ways of earning a living,' shuddered the captain, as a bridge-wing door was hurriedly closed against the raw blast.

The scientific base is a motley and tight cluster of buildings. Low-roofed wooden structures, rendered rock-like by the rigours of climate, abut a large two-storey fibreglass unit. Neat rows of square windows and the hint of a normal lifestyle within belied its location. Lying off the small jetty, a modern cabined workboat lay at its mooring. To this incongruous scene the three penguins and slumbering seal added the bizarre finishing touches.

As a permanent station, Signy needs occasional transfusions of its lifeblood to sustain occupancy. Chosen by the eye of necessity, the large fuel tank sat separate and bold on an adjacent slope. Raised on trestle legs, a pipeline undulated shorewards, linking to a green umbilical, flaked out for connection to the ship. Kept afloat by empty rusting oil drums, the pipe was towed out and pulled aboard at the stern. In total, 140 tonnes of fuel were pumped to the tank, a process which took many hours and demanded laborious attention at ship and shore. In the pristine environment was the ever-present need to avoid the slightest pollution. The base is also an unusual location for a post office. Here, letters are greedily stamped as originating from this outpost in the British Antarctic Territories.

Her task of landing boxed airfreight completed, the launch was free to attend to liberty duties. There were plenty of passengers, all eager to visit the islands for many reasons. Some sought shelter in the bar with old friends; others took to wandering the nearby rocky paths, anxious to capture nuances of the island and its sense of place. From the summit cairn of Cemetery Hill, the sense of place was profound, making the elevation and the effort to achieve its vantage well worth it. The cove was a shapely foreground, the scientific base and tethered ship diminutive in the order of scale. Their presence seemed natural, complementary to the sweeping panorama beyond: to the peaks of Coronation Island across Iceberg Bay; the smooth radiant expanse of Sunshine Glacier and the darker hinterland of Signy, its own heights shrouded in cloud.

Such heady glimpses were not available to all. On the ship's after deck, attendance to small details kept eyes lowered. The tide was receding towards low water. Over the ship's stern the leadline was lowered to assess the depth remaining. It levelled off at the final ebb with 3 feet of clearance below the keel.

Colin was a learner driver. At least that was how his crew-mates viewed him, and they had been mischievously busy behind the scenes on his behalf. Taking the afternoon shift at helming the liberty launch, he was initiated

Refuelling Signy base via floating
pipeline. (Author's collection)

Caution! Learner driver at the
helm...! (Author's collection)

into the quirks of the boat's character. He could but laugh at the attentions of his colleagues. They had thoughtfully provided a huge L-plate, which obliterated half of the cabin.

Half of my own cabin seemed buried on my return, beneath a bounty of chocolate bars. A small mystery, it was a gift from the base to all aboard. Their stocks were abundant, but the use-by date was imminent. Such mutual generosity was set aside for the formalities of paperwork. The provision of fuel was a matter of moment. Reassured by a tank refilled, the base could withstand an enforced overwintering if the schedule of *John Biscoe*'s later visit could not be met.

It was time to take our leave and attend once more to the current itinerary. The hum of activity again centred on the ship, the scientists turned linesmen for the second time in a day. The stiff breeze was constantly abrasive, seeking new ways to hinder. On the exposed bow, the chief officer crouched low to keep the voice of the wind away from his radio. It was a slow business bringing in the long head-ropes, hauling at the slow but regular pace of the revolving winch drums. A slight heel had mysteriously appeared, the ship leaning very slightly off the vertical. It was an irony against the care of the engineers, in the discharge of their transfer of fuel to the shore.

They had set the ship bolt upright with their final dispositions of fuel, but were thwarted at the last. As the launch was hoisted and stowed on the port side, her weight tipped the balance. In soft tones, the chief engineer muttered a mild expletive, a polite and jovial aside at the quip of fate that was noticeable to only a few. The giving of hand signals was reversed, a shorthand of language between foredeck and bridge, as the anchors were weighed. The captain acknowledged each gesture with a slight nod, as if making an auction bid. As the second anchor broke free of its grip and hung aweigh, the ship gathered speed, making her exit with a flourish of style. The blasts of her whistle bade farewell, answered by red rocket flares from the shore. On the radio, a high-pitched and demented rendering of 'We'll meet again' yodelled across the airwaves. No sooner were we gone than there were thoughts of the return.

Exercising his powers of humour, without seeking an audience, an off-duty seaman walked the length of the alleyway. It was an amusing trick, being able to apparently lean his be-towelled body from one side to the other, without falling over. In reality, the ship's rolling motion provided the hidden means. It was simply an act of balance to stay vertical that gave the illusion of defying gravity. Intent purely on having a hot shower, the swaying motion would still need due care in case a slip turned into a bone-breaking disaster. Padding barefoot back to his cabin, wet footprints lingered as a telltale trail.

The sprucing up of the ship had been evident all the next morning. Extra care was lavished by the stewards in their work as proud housekeepers. Crew cabins found their occupants directing this weekly attention with an eye to finer detail. Some needed the excuse; others saw it as a reward. The captain's weekly inspection was approaching. It was a Sunday morning event, recorded in the ship's log: 'Master's inspection of accommodation, store-rooms and galley.' An official requirement, the task was carried out with due accord.

Accompanied by the chief officer and catering officer, their collective rounds acknowledged the running and maintenance of the interior, picking up on defects and exchanging pleasantries with the crew. None feared the absurdity of a white-gloved finger drawn along the door tops, a lore out of a bygone age, but neither was it a cursory scan. Important places took their share of scrutiny. The walk-in stores and cold rooms were opened to have their controlled interiors inspected.

The wider world also pressed in on us. A clinging fog absorbed the watchkeeper's eyes in its grey myopic void. On to its blank neutrality the imagination could print its pictures, in defiance of logic; hidden icebergs overlapped with the faces of distant loved ones; happy moments of holidays jostled with the unknown, just beyond sight. My evening reverie out of the bridge windows recalled the glimpse of Clarence Island. Was it to be only a radar image, in passing? The warning was subliminal: something was happening to the dusk. Within a ship's length *John Biscoe* had emerged from the fog into a startling clarity and stillness. Looking astern, the wall of vapour extended to that longed-for and silvery horizon.

Clarence Island was a shock. It dominated the northern prospect; immediate, as if painted on the very windows. To the watercolourist it would have been a glorious study in Payne's grey, a tonal spectrum from heavy brooding cloud to the pale glow of snowy peaks, and the forms of icebergs intervening. Some moments are meant only for memory. My relief at midnight smiled at my recollections, as he remembered similar moments from the store of his own experience. They came to link us in a navigators' bond, the slow-flowering growth of shared understanding that can turn acquaintance into friendship.

***

Year's end: on the last day of December, the resolution was made to make amends and clear the decks of work outstanding. James Ross Island beckoned. The fog was stoically endured because of the north wind. This was regarded as a helping hand. It was hoped that it had urged the ice south, to make a clear passage. Gaining the northern approach to Antarctic Sound called once more for disciplined navigation. There were no guide marks as lavished on the coasts of congested commercial trade routes. Buoys, lighthouses, and the many other features of civilisation to be grasped and used by the canny navigator were missing. Fundamentals were called upon, as was flexibility in their use.

A radar screen filled with targets can daunt the observer. Switching to a shorter range is a trick to fool the mind. As an orienteer keeps to his intended course despite obstructions to his path, each deviation in the ship's course was compensated, returning to the prime line. The wind of change came as a mixed blessing. It dispelled the fog and enabled a wider appreciation of the panorama. Enthusiastic observers crowded the bridge top, multicoloured in their warm garments. A beacon to all, the twin-pronged peak of Mount Bransfield proclaimed the very tip of the Trinity Peninsula. It was a sight to inspire and raise hopes, but the wind played devil's advocate. As realisation dawned, a silence fell. The wind blew from the south; with it came the prospect of ice.

Antarctic Sound proved to be blocked by ice. The ship lingered at its edge, as yet more decisions hung in the balance. Prudence prevailed: on the night of New Year there could be no better place to anchor than Hope Bay. A sense of isolation was tempered, for here was another outpost of humanity. The permanent settlement registered as a pattern of regular dots beneath the backdrop of high mountains and sweeping glacier. The red wooden buildings grew in detail with our approach to the bay. Within its confines, navigation marks had indeed been erected. On Grunden Rock a stubby latticed yellow tower carried a flashing light, held above the grounded ice and shielded in the cusp of an ice cliff beyond. Our neighbours were Argentinian, their radioed Spanish greeting interpreted and duly answered. Nationality crumbled with the generosity of free spirits.

Maintaining our own temporary residence was no easy matter, and it was brought up to anchor in the sheltered off-lying waters. A land breeze kept the ship pointing shorewards. Responding to the eddies of the tide, the brash ice sailed in defiance of the wind. In a lazy circulation they toured the bay, a slowly swirling armada. Some bumped harmlessly along the hull, but an adversary had seen its chance. A large floe with hooked end latched its claw around our bow. With nonchalant ease it dragged the *John Biscoe* with it, anchor and all. Escape and re-anchoring was an unlooked-for tedium.

Keeping watch on the bridge, New Year's night was as cold as the revelling spirits were warm. The sounds of their partying suffused the wheelhouse through the open inner door, borne by the heated air from below. It helped augment the output from the hard-pressed radiator towards which the seat of my long johns was directed.

The top of the tide came and went; the grounded ice nearby did not float off to cause problems. The only movement was the gentle yaw of the ship as she rode to anchor. A solitary figure moved slowly from one red hut to another, the only sign of life. At the chart table, an animated conference was in session. Higher authorities discussed plans for the next day, weather permitting. Time was getting short and a move would need to be made soon. Scattered across the table, learned tomes and resurrected charts were all consulted.

Across the airwaves a Spanish voice also made enquiry. Once more summoned as interpreter, the electrician shamed us into admiring smiles as his easy banter played the careful diplomat. Their invitation to join the celebrations ashore was politely insistent. In an exposed anchorage, the crew could not be safely dispersed. A gentle assertiveness declined the kind offer.

At midnight the ship's company seemed happy to congregate at the bow, a milling throng parading forward, to sing out and ring in the New Year. To *John Biscoe*'s bell went the honour of announcing 1991. The refreshing message rang clearly as cheers erupted and the spray of cider was broadcast at the sky. Like comradely confetti it fell on the heads of the crew, scientists and officers.

'Happy New Year!' said the second officer into the radio. The Argentinians replied: 'Yes – we are very 'appy…'

CHAPTER 3

Logistics in Action

Hopes confounded – Establishing field stations – Return to the Falkland Islands.

On the first day of January the weather seemed benign enough to attempt a second run into Fridtjof Sound. Leaving the Argentinian settlement in Hope Bay behind, the ship edged through the icy obstructions. Cloud cover was breaking and it showed all the signs of becoming a classic day of Antarctic summer. Becoming 'dinglified' was the unscientific but graphic term for such welcome improvement.

The north end of the Sound was mostly clear of ice, an effective lure to the gaping jaws at its southern exit. Between the east flanking islands of Jonassen and Anderssen, currents met with the main tidal stream, creating a smooth cauldron of swirling eddies which jostled the ship disconcertingly. Concentrations of penguins porpoised and dived, revealing the grace of their underwater flight. On passing ice floes their companions scurried, decorum abandoned, flapping furiously as they tobogganed to watery safety, escaping the looming red bulk of the ship above them.

Eventually meeting some pack ice, the ship rode up, and split and nudged her way through, leaving the scuffed red paint marks of battle on the scarred ice edges. Halfway through the Sound, a vista of impenetrable pack ice stretched to the horizon. Described as ten-tenths concentration, it was a dazzling white terrain of contorted and alien design. Borne down towards its leading edge by the now following tide, it was a difficult task to turn the ship away from its clutches. The dark bulk of our hoped-for destination could be seen 20 miles distant – comparatively so near, yet so very far away.

So near, yet so far: 'Ten-tenths' ice, compacted by currents and wind in Fridtjof Sound, denies access to James Ross Island. (Author's collection)

Resigned to the inaccessibility of James Ross Island the alternative plan was adopted. Once again, it was the best operational compromise.

After several miles of backtracking, following the western coastal trend of the Tabarin Peninsula, the sheltered bay below Brown Bluff was reached. On the slow speed approach, the sonar pinged its angled searching beam forward. At regular intervals, positions were plotted, and corrected echo sounder depths noted and marked on the hitherto largely blank chart. There was plenty of scope for original hydrography, to add to the accumulation of information gleaned throughout the years by the Survey's vessels.

The forbidding hard-edged ice cliffs ended abruptly, contrasting with the warm hues of the craggy pinnacle mass of Brown Bluff, rising well in excess of 2,000 feet. This was to be the location and area of study for a small field station which was about to be established. Utter calm had settled; the sea was a mirrored surface, broken by the boats that sped the two-man party ashore. There was plenty of help in setting up the station and providing the necessities for eight weeks of isolation in such harsh splendour.

Smitten by an untimely bug that had been doing the rounds of the ship I was told that I looked like death. Taking the pills prescribed by the doctor, I declined to operate one of the shore boats, relinquishing the pleasure to John. We each had the best of both worlds: he, an afternoon of boat-work in idyllic conditions, escaping anchor watch; I, to several hours of blissful oblivion snug beneath the duvet, escaping the misery of my ailment.

Illness on a ship is always a real bugbear. Necessarily, shipboard routine is relentless, as are the demands on crew, such that malady almost becomes taboo.

* * *

Good time was made overnight in traversing the Bransfield Strait, although the approach to the anchorage off the Byers Peninsula was something of a navigational headache for the chief officer. Early calls and breakfasts had been arranged, as the day was to start promptly at eight o'clock. Looking out of the wardroom window at Livingston Island, the King Fid exclaimed to a colleague in quiet despair, 'I've never seen so much snow on this God-forsaken hole.' He seemed less than overjoyed at the prospect of geological studies in such conditions, and this was compounded by disappointment at not being able to reach the primary goal of James Ross Island.

At seven o'clock the crew made ready two of the inflatables. Two three-man crews had been chosen. A chart and hand compass provided safety cover in relocating the ship, should the weather close in. The aim of the landing was to establish an advance camp depot in an area remote from the intended main station.

On the ship's derrick a net-load of cargo hung poised over the side. In the rising lop the inflatable was carefully edged beneath, as we were aware of the potential for its crew being crushed. Cargo aboard, it was covered with a protective canvas sheet. The equipment would arrive on shore in better condition than the boat crew. For the best part of an hour, the boats kept company, making slow and soaking passage into wind and sea, laden low in the water and sluggish in response to the waves. Quickly drenched and with the bite of chill water seeping down necks and eventually arriving at underclothes and wellingtons, the best form of defence was masochistic laughter, and teasing the bedraggled state of everyone else. Tucked up towards the bow, back against the onslaught, Sue was candidly philosophical about her freezing nether garments.

Slowly *John Biscoe* receded, the boats eventually heading towards shore, lining up a reference point on a notable rock bluff. Finding a landing place in the blustery conditions was not easy, as we encountered rocky shoals and smooth humps which reluctantly materialised into basking elephant seals. By mutual aid, a landing was achieved and the heavy boats hauled sufficiently up the beach. The labour of carrying the miscellaneous packages of rucksacks, wooden boxes and tents, at least temporarily, warmed our constitutions.

On a rocky mound beyond high tide mark, the cache was stockpiled, covered overall with a black tarpaulin, and carefully tucked and weighted round with many stones. The outcrop showed signs of previous human use. Stones in artificial configuration betrayed to experienced eyes the remnant of an old sealers' hut. On this day the elephant seals were unperturbed by human presence.

Fortified with high-energy victuals, a speedy and more comfortable return trip was anticipated, and so it proved. In twenty minutes the boats were back aboard. The crews looked forward to peeling off the dank but life-preserving clothes, and to fully appreciating the simple luxury of a hot shower.

Later on, conditions deteriorated. An assessment was made as to the viability of transporting the heavier and bulky equipment for the main field station. The towing launch and cargo-laden barge, known as the scow, would need careful handling at ship and shore, and on passage. With time in hand, it was decided to wait for improvement, as early mornings often provide the best conditions. The ship relaxed into a routine of normality, a breathing space in the pace of events to catch up on matters set aside: writing letters, model making, doing the ironing.

On the bridge the watchman carried out his modified duties while the ship was at anchor. For clarity these were written by the chief officer:

January 2nd/3rd:
Off Vietor Rocks, Byers Peninsula, Livingston Island.
Starboard anchor, 4 shackles. Turn wheel 20 degrees each way, every 20 minutes.
Call Duty Officer if:-
1. Wind speed reaches a steady 35 knots.
2. If vessel appears to be, or is, dragging anchor.
3. Radar is on the picture plot; range ring set on Vietor Rock.
4. If in any doubt whatsoever.

Calls: Cooks and stewards as normal.
Chief Officer 0445. Deck crew 0530 for 0600 turn-to, subject to weather etc.
Make hourly fire patrols.

* * *

Once again plans were thwarted by conditions, the sea state for small open craft being unworkable. Getting the ship nearer to the main site was the solution. It was only a distance of some 5 miles between anchorages, but 60 miles of steaming and a first-ever approach to that particular location. Snow Island, off-lying dangers and the unnavigable

Morton Strait between it and Livingston Island were the several causes of the prolonged passage. Good use was made of the occasion, to derive more hydrographic data. It was a process that the chief officer revelled in, enjoying the graphic complexity of processing the carefully collated numerical results that would eventually enable a new run of soundings to be plotted on the chart. Most of that work would come later, in quiet periods. For Robin it was a change from the material realities of managing the ship's logistical programme. Sharp pencils and fine-tipped pens were plied well into the night, with a pleasurable accuracy, on the lamp-lit chart table. The end result was a satisfying line of many neatly spaced numbers, arranged like sleepers on a railway track, across the virgin blank terrain of chart.

Weighing up the options. Captain Elliott often had to make difficult operational decisions in response to changing ice and weather conditions. (Author's collection)

Snow Island itself was too distant to see in the laden air. Eddystone Rocks and Rugged Island were the first to appear, one on either bow. As the depth reduced, our speed correspondingly reduced. Our approach into New Plymouth Sound was an original exercise. 'The first run in is always the worst,' reflected the captain. Conning the vessel, with verbal information supplied from operators at the sonar, radar and echo sounder, navigation oozed under pressure from beneath the closed bridge doors, enveloping the quiet observers outside with a mystical aura to match the unfolding prospect. A grounded iceberg guarded the entrance to the Sound, fashioning the mellowing light which bathed it into changing forms. At evening, when viewed from the anchorage, its twin bulk appeared convincingly as a yacht in full sail, living dangerously by crossing the bow of a looming steamer.

Beneath the towering pinnacle cliffs of the eastern extremity of Rugged Island, the ship was finally brought up dramatically to anchor. Across the Sound lay the Byers Peninsula, shaped like a clawed hand petrified in the act of snatching at Rugged Island. Within its grasp it held low snow-covered slopes, fringed offshore with outrunning reefs towards Astor Island and the irregular jutting teeth of Stewart Stacks. In the ensuing boat operations to shore, two of these were a godsend, as leading marks to guide the craft safely through the hazards.

With lunchtime disrupted by the midday arrival, it was with satisfied appetites that the crews headed their boats obliquely towards the shore, two red splashes of vibrant life that spun a speedy white thread of wake in their passing. Their task: to scout the area for a suitable approach and landing. Initially hopes were high at being able to land the equipment with the launch and scow. Neatly stacked one inside the other, these robust craft occupied one side of the well deck. The scow was flat bottomed and slab sided, designed to maximise carrying capacity. There was no compromise in its angular form or function, no consideration to sea-kindliness or ease of manoeuvring.

In the peaceful warmth of the bridge the gripping progress of the scouts could be heard on the VHF radio. It was not to be plain sailing. The nature of the reefs was becoming evident; so too the ensnaring trap of dense kelp at the shore, hiding isolated submerged rocks. One of these shattered a propeller to fragments. A quick-fit replacement and the necessary tools were stowed under the canopy for just such an eventuality. It was an impossibility to use the larger craft for the operation. 'Life is but a shambles,' sighed King Fid Mike, in the face of the dampened expectations of his long-frustrated scientific colleagues.

In the 'tween deck hold, the cargo brooded large, mutely insistent on being moved, somehow. It fell to the indomitable inflatable boats, and was a lengthy task spiced with incident. Two scow loads equated to thirty-five round trips of the smaller craft. In a spirit of eager enthusiasm the orange covers were removed from all three boats. Crews appeared resplendent in padded floatation suits of bright red, nicknamed Bertie Bassetts because of the coloured rings of reflective tape about arms and legs. Hard, green toecaps of safety wellingtons protruded while an ear-muffed hard hat crowned each head. A waistcoat lifejacket completed the attire.

Launched by the crane, the three boats lay in readiness. It was a water level world for them, subject to each whim of wave and wind. To the long swell the ship lifted and dipped lazily as the undulation of waves ran from stem to stern. Looking upwards from the boats, each net of equipment blocked the sky as it was slung outboard. A hand clung to a steadying rope, the other reached up to grasp and control the descending load. The dynamic lop jostled the boat beneath the poise of cargo. There was little room left in the boat, only sufficient to steer and to provide a cramped space for the crew. With cargo hook released, rearranging began. Wooden cases and metal boxes sat quietly, the lengthy tents of the initial loads were awkward. Provisions, fuel, scientific equipment, snow shoes, ice axes; all took their turn.

Again sluggish with the weight, the boats set off in loose convoy. As pioneers they picked and prospected their way through a confusion of reefs, seeking the islets to bring into line, as a guide for the run towards the shore. Paddles out, the shallows were probed, the weedy mats eyed with suspicion. Draped thickly over the shoreline boulders, the kelp softened the landfall, nosing into padded clefts to the hiss and threat of elephant seals. As a defence against our bridgehead they gaped their lurid bloodshot mouths. Some advanced with effective menace. We were invading their hallowed place of repose.

It was an unconventional form of stevedoring, to offload the stores in such terrain. As the boats regained a sufficient depth to lower the outboard engines, they left the first party to sample the isolation. Our return to the ship would be swift. For the present free of encumbrance, the boats forged a dizzy passage back to the ship, each bowman hanging on with grim enjoyment as the bucking craft rose and fell. In the stern, the helmsman at least felt more in control of his fate, in playing the confusion of waves that reared before him.

Two loads safely delivered in boat JB4, her crew felt a growing confidence. Things were going well, then the cruel cut came. It had been a distant half-thought that the next descending load seemed overly large, but that was not the real threat. Lurking with sharp-edged menace, a barbed corner lay undetected. 'Lower away,' brought a sickening expulsion of air as the cargo

Inflatable boats were used to establish and remove a temporary scientific field station on Livingston Island, in the South Shetlands. (Author's collection)

Elephant seals were an added complication to an already challenging landfall during the protracted task of establishing the field station on Livingston Island. (Author's collection)

slumped into the boat. With the decisive accuracy of a surgeon's scalpel, one flank of the inflatable was incised. Loss of buoyancy was immediate. In its wounded state the boat limped round to be lifted aboard.

On the tiled deck in the laboratory, JB4 was spreadeagled like a collapsed tent. Beneath the lights the tear was swabbed and examined. On hands and knees, the ever-adaptable captain enjoyed this non-executive task. On the bench beside his glass of beer, the tools were arranged: scissors, emery cloth, adhesive, rubber patches and hairdryer. Before they too had been hoisted aboard for the night, the remaining boats had also diced with the fates. The engine of JB1 had become troublesome. JB2 almost flipped over on its final exuberant return. Messing about in boats always provides a bounty for cabin yarns, some of which will be embellished into legends.

Most of the shore party spent their first night at base camp, sufficient equipment having been landed the previous day to allow for a comfortable rest. From the distant vantage point of the ship, the tepee-shaped tents could just be discerned, as regular dots breaking into the monotony of a snow bank beyond their chosen site, a level plain above the area of beach. In erecting their orange canvas dwellings they had chosen to face the circular entrances westward, towards the sea.

The VHF radio jumped to life as morning contact was made. Tide and sea conditions were relayed as the clearing of early mist was awaited. Yet again the Humber inflatables were to prove their worth in no uncertain terms. At early breakfast they were spoken of with quiet affection. Ever associated with *John Biscoe*, they were due to be withdrawn at the end of the season, after nine voyages in the Antarctic. In that lingering reference of years, what was left unsaid spoke volumes about the boats' endurance. Returned to health, JB4 was back on its cradle. On its inner flank a repair patch of brilliant orange was worn with swelling pride, like a healed battle scar.

The three boats made fourteen heavily laden runs to shore in the morning. A brisk sea and swell were running, thankfully from ship to shore. By lunchtime the tide had dropped to unworkable levels at the beach, its off-lying shallows a morass of choking kelp. Taking a breather allowed time to take stock. Ashore, unpacking and tallying continued. Aboard, more net loads were assembled in readiness. Engines thirsty for fuel, the supply was renewed. Careful mixing of lubricant and hand-pumping of the petrol from the red-topped drum were absorbing tasks in the pleasant afternoon sun.

The finale was to begin after dinner. As the last of the shore party still on board, Mike and Sue indulged in the prospect of taking their 'last shower', and to relishing the pampered comfort of their 'last meal' in the wardroom. The decision hung in the balance, as the swirling mist once again held the starting gun. At the stage when cheese and biscuits were being sampled, the word filtered through, sending a palpable wave of energy through the ship: 'It's on!'

As if responding to a scramble, activity became feverish. For Sue, having relinquished her former position as an instructor at an Outward Bound centre, the reason she had elected to be in Antarctica had begun to dawn. Finished in her role as a patient tally clerk in the ship's hold, overseeing the departure of equipment, the job of specialist support beckoned. She and the other GAs would be able to flex their skills in alpine and mountaineering crafts and survival.

The eleven remaining journeys took nearly three hours. There was surprise when the bosun advised that two more runs would see all the cargo dispatched. It had become like a way of life: no end was contemplated. The chief scientist gave his generous thanks and farewells. If all went to plan he would next see us from the quay at Grimsby to witness *John Biscoe*'s final arrival home in the UK. The newly established field station would be visited once in the following weeks by the Royal Naval ice patrol ship, HMS *Endurance*. In the meantime, assembled as an independent unit, they would quickly become a tight working community. They launched their intentions with raised glasses, filled with the nectar known as Rumbo Jumbo, a generous warming elixir with rum as its essence. Diminutive in its panorama, *John Biscoe* spent her last night at anchor. In the dawn hours she sailed beyond sight.

* * *

The passing days were marked by subtle milestones. Referring to a blank calendar is little use in determining if it is Sunday or Thursday. Crossing off the days is taboo: it stirs untimely thoughts and notions of wishing life away. There are many other pointers that more subtly mark the progress of time. At midnight, page turning in the logbooks heralds the first recording of a new day. It is also registered at the top of each menu. Fridays are marked by a lunch of fish, chips and mushy peas. On Monday mornings the paper on the barograph drum is changed. Saturday is more generally recognised as the day of the engineers' weekly tests.

The ritual opening of a fire hydrant at the foredeck entrance was the first sign. Shortly afterwards, as if by voluntary act, the hydrant spumed out an aerated torrent, darkly staining the bleached wooden deck before cascading over the side or fussing into the scupper pipes. Deep within the ship's bows two engineers tested the emergency fire pump. Intent on low-key mayhem they continued their noise-making activities elsewhere. With forewarning, a wailing siren echoed through the cluttered cavern of the engine room: the alarm for the CO_2 fire-smothering system. The emergency generator chimed in with its decibels in distant vocal exchange with a lifeboat engine. The ship's crew was in no doubt when Saturday morning had arrived.

Watchkeepers are blamed for much. They are occasionally credited with small miracles. In either case it is a traditional and largely good-humoured presumption. Weather conditions are a favourite. 'Where on earth did you get this mank from?' or 'this isn't what we ordered' are two of the more polite comments.

At evening meal relief, the chief officer leaned close to the bridge window, intent in his frustration on sending a penetrating gaze through his sunglasses out into the fog. He was chafing at the bit. Such visibility was tedious, a dampener to progress. At reduced speed the ship groped forward. Lone growlers were always at the back of the mind; the hands of the clock moved reluctantly. Clinging to the shadowed bridge-wing a ghostly phenomenon hovered mysteriously in a tight arc. The weak sun, perversely shining through the fog from the opposite side painted this Brocken spectre, a glowing silvery ring imposed on the pale blanket behind. It was a rare spectacle, to be recorded in the Met. Log, yet seen without enthusiasm. A sharp horizon with good visibility had been ordered.

At meal break I took up the chief officer's stance at the window, as he gratefully went below for dinner. A stray reflection on the glass jolted the heart. Directly ahead I had seen a phantom iceberg. No, this visibility would never do! Unwittingly I performed the miracle: the fog dissipated and with it the spectre. I sensed admiration from the lookout in the corner. I eased forward on the speed control. The satisfying response of power would be felt throughout the ship. I basked in the occasion, awaiting the credit that was surely mine.

'Well done, Trevor,' I heard from Robin, now satisfied in more than appetite, as he drank in the panoramic seascape. It was a short-lived tonic, as the fog closed in once again. On taking over the watch at eight o'clock, I anticipated no more miracles, but rather a thickening of the gloom. Floating by were the sad remains of an albatross that had given up its wandering spirit, and, as a timely scapegoat, it was given the wider blame.

As daylight faded, the ship's navigation lights enhanced the feeling of being cocooned, as their glow scattered back from the diffusing fog, casting an eerie twilight of uneasy beauty. The radar screen was viewed with care, blank but for the central smudge from the encircling waves. On the hour, the lookout changed. Emerging from below, Martin reported that all was quiet. He relieved David, who told him that there was nothing about, adding dryly that he was not likely to see anything either. In my turn I was to leave John at midnight to his graveyard watch until 4 a.m., where small miracles can pass unseen.

In this region, observing the radar screen to detect other ships offers frugal reward. More used to congested seas, a quiet pining seasoned my inspections of screen and horizon. Ships offer a focus for attention, an excuse to grapple for the bulky binoculars in their deep box, to see a mirror of ourselves pass beneath the patterned vastness of sky. Earlier in the day, beyond the range of vision or radar, a friend had passed, Antarctic-bound from the Falklands to which we were now returning. Known affectionately as the Encumbrance, the ice patrol ship HMS *Endurance* had been in radio contact. Plotting her position, she proved to be 90 miles to the south. As a naval vessel, she was unable to relay her intentions, but her charted track suggested a destination of Smith Island or the Boyd Strait, at the western extremity of the South Shetlands.

As our southerly latitude decreased with our northward passage, the nights were becoming more apparent. Agreeing with the lookout's sentiment and welcoming proper darkness for a change, I added to myself, only if there's no ice. It was folly, presuming to maintain a quick passage and arrive early, yet we seemed unstoppable. Even a brisk headwind and regular marching sea did not falter our speed or affect our comfort. Showing contempt at our delight the wind increased in the early hours to a gale that urged the sea to rise like a buffeting wall. In defeat, our speed was duly cut by half, the passage now laboured and doused with spray. With 150 miles to go we watched our arrival time recede alarmingly, yet adjusted with a seaman's acceptance to the new reality.

In such weather the bridge became a viewing gallery for spectators. Assuming a resigned interest, eyes peered forward at the turmoil. Cameras emerged and the stalking of a particular scene ensued. As if suddenly shy of attention, the sea ceased its excessive commotion. 'Where's a big wave when you want one?' asked David in exasperation, his little camera poised across the bridge-wing dodger. Inevitably the best moment occurs just after the shutter is pressed. As with capturing leaping dolphins, it is a frustrating goal.

Through this area of ill-intent, dubbed the Falklands Wallow Zone, thoughts of land inspired the captain to an action he had considered earlier. Self-critical for not sticking to his guns and newly armed with the latest weather information, he wielded dividers and parallel rule on the chart. Smiling with triumph he swung the ship's course a full 30° off the wind. 'We're going tacking,' he announced. 'We must get out of the habit of always pointing the way we want to go.' On powered vessels the ability to progress straight into wind and seas is often clung to with blinkered reverence. Tacking either side of the wind, as sailing ships had to do, can offer surprising advantages. Gone were the heavy head seas, now moved on to one shoulder. Through these artificially lengthened seas the ship rode more comfortably, less prone to shuddering stops or a racing propeller. Speed was increased dramatically, more than compensating for the extra distance incurred. Our required arrival time for the restricted port entry was no longer impossible, just agonisingly borderline. It was hoped, as on other occasions, that it was not to be 'so near yet so far'.

Throughout the afternoon our modified track was followed, and we gained quieter waters in the lee of the Falklands. The expected wind-shift came, bringing clearer skies of friendly aspect. Altering once again towards our destination of Cape Pembroke we found a following sea which bowled the ship along in a fashion proper for an exuberant landfall. Such was the good humour that when the long blast and continuous ringing of alarm bells summoned the company to boat drill, it was attended in jovial mood.

On the boat deck the lifeboats sat innocently between their tall launching arms. Of a type known as luffing davits they were a minor headache to swing outboard, in comparison with modern gravity davits. These would have made *John Biscoe* top heavy so her originals remained as exercise for their launch parties in deployment and recovery. Those at life raft stations had it easy and lent a hand in turning the heavy cranks that inched their bulky loads across the deck.

The black-and-white banded lighthouse on Cape Pembroke stood proudly at the end of its low jut of land. Between it and the off-lying Seal Rocks, conditions allowed for a timely shortcut for the ship to bear into the large inlet of Port William, the outer approach to Stanley. Swinging west towards its interior the crew directed their gazes shoreward, pausing in their task of getting the ropes up and coiling them neatly on deck.

The proper way to any island is by sea. A month previously the fast convenience of air travel had brought this stranger to the Falklands in a clinical technology that denied appreciation. In pale silhouette on the horizon the islands' slow growth from our seaward approach allowed for peaceful contemplation. It felt like a proper introduction. I was arriving not as a complete stranger as before, but as a returning visitor with time to explore. In that same month I had explored new territories within myself, in the role of working on a highly unusual and individual vessel in very new and challenging surroundings. A lot of water had passed beneath the keel and reflected the internal sea change that made me feel at home. I, too, looked towards the shore with pleasant anticipation.

The main entrance through into Stanley harbour keeps itself hidden to the last. At a mooring buoy, the British warship HMS *Cumberland* lay broadside. It was an opportunity for a maritime courtesy and the exercise of flag etiquette. Considering it unseemly to sweep past at full speed, Captain Elliott eased back on the control, also adjusting the rake of his white cap for the occasion. At a dignified pace we passed close by as ensigns were dutifully dipped – lowered and raised – in a traditional show of preening. Mutual waves were exchanged before the business at hand was resumed.

The sunlit colours of evening caught the many painted hues of the dwellings in Stanley, as if they too were exhibiting the bunting of welcome. Edging towards her allotted berth, the starboard anchor was let go. A pivotal restraining influence to drive against it held the bow away from the floating quay, allowing the stern to swing as required; this was a deft and well-tried manoeuvre for those appreciative eyes waiting in the shelter of the grey metalled warehouses.

Heaving lines were thrown from the ship, given momentum by the bunched 'monkey's fist' at their ends. Wary of their descending punch the shore linesmen watched these unravelling coils snake overhead, ready to snatch and tame them. It is a source of scorn to let these rope envoys slither back into the water, under the hard gaze of the crew that threw them. Thus the heavy mooring ropes were hauled to the bollards. Eased into position alongside, the 'crossed forearms' signal relayed the message to make fast. At the stern the second officer was enthusiastic with the number of ropes used, as he reported, 'Four stern-lines and two springs secure.' In appreciative and light-hearted response the following remark was made: 'Has John been knitting again?'

In the approaches to Stanley, as *John Biscoe* slowly passes the moored HMS *Cumberland*, Captain Elliott prepares to exchange traditional courtesy greetings. (Author's collection)

CHAPTER 4

Endeavours for Ocean Biology

Busy times at Port Stanley – Hunting for krill – South Georgia.

Stanley was *John Biscoe*'s true home port, as registered beneath her name at the stern; this was the reason why her ensign was that of the Falklands. It seemed an unusual place for such an attachment, yet there was no denying the span of her connection. As a globe-trotting but local resident, she was accepted as such, a periodic facet of life to draw the local gaze, raised eyes acknowledging the return of a well-known face. Among the stationery in a gift shop, a postcard of the ship betrayed an affectionate and unspoken pride.

Local people were wont to come aboard at invitation and find hospitality in the crew bar. Home it may have been for the ship; it was a different home for those aboard, who would lock their cabins behind them. So, too, the bridge was made secure, the door key secreted in its allotted nook. Fresh voices echoed along the alleyways, replacing the silence of a ship brought to rest. New faces appeared around corners or on stairwells. They were greeted as old friends. The sole agent of the British Antarctic Survey in the Falklands, Myrium was a key figure. She was plied with questions in plenty, and had plenty to tell.

Hopes and expectations for mail were met in varying degrees. For those where none had arrived there would be a sinking disappointment, a wound to their brittle self-sufficiency. Equilibrium is unsettled and the imagination runs riot, but tempered with insistent reasoning that all is well. More mail would be brought by the scientists due to join next day.

In Stanley and its environs there was no feeling of homesickness, despite its obvious reminders of Scotland. Ever a magnetic source of inspiration, I was drawn ashore, and keen to go. There was plenty of activity on the ship but it was my turn to cash in the favours. With a ready generosity John urged me to take my dues.

I was advised of the shore path to Stanley, which was more interesting than the road; it can't be missed. Armed with the ability to overlook the obvious I did manage to find the desired pathway off the stony roadside, towards a simple stile. I smiled at my surprise. What sort of vegetation had I expected to see? Clearly something exotic, something uniquely of the southern hemisphere; yet the path was bedecked with swaying grasses with familiar seed-heads, clovers, dandelions and stands of flowering gorse. Yellow lichens clothed the rocks above the tide mark; and were those sparrows I saw?

I would be forgiven for calling Stanley harbour a Scottish sea loch, likening the township to a faraway Ullapool, for instance. Hemispheres linked within the mind's compass enhanced my exploration and discoveries. The houses were certainly individual, wooden and functional, brightened with colours, some of doubtful coordination. On a fence, a bold black whale grinned at me beneath the message 'Say No to Whaling'. These were common signs, nailed up as symbols to changed times, in contrast to the whalebone arches that reared within the grounds of the cathedral.

Life seemed parochial and self-contained until the reminders of recent conflicts jarred the memory. Beyond the town the recent war memorial stood, with names cast in bronze, and the inscription 'In memory of those who liberated us'.

A liberty bus ran a regular service between the ship and town, keeping Bob the driver busy. Unfailingly polite to his fellow citizens he would raise a casual hand in greeting many times during the day, often to a silhouette behind the wheel of a passing Land Rover. These vehicles seemed the norm. To have an ordinary car would appear eccentric.

Such a word might describe the opening times of shops and facilities. The locals could not rightly tell if the far-off museum would be open. Even advertised hours were subject to whim, a regular afternoon opening vetoed by a week's closure, leaving a frustrated tourist on the doorstep, soft toy penguins unreachable beyond the green shutters. They stored the wool in the back room of Past Times. Armed with orders from the knitters back home, who were familiar with the qualities of the Falklands product, the burden of choosing the ply and colours fell to an inexpert eye. By summer, and half a world away, hand-knitted cardigans would be paraded, exclusively of wool specially delivered from a far-off land. Suddenly my old wallet was very empty, all the shore-sub gone.

I had set the alarm clock to wake me early the next morning. Beyond the thick curtains was daylight. At sea, drawing them back was frequently a disciplined act. Beyond their cocooning warmth was the real world. Opening them affirmed the intention of emerging from the cabined privacy, the safe world of being off duty. In port, and with a morning free for self-indulgence, it was a delicious surprise to be greeted by a calm prospect and beckoning sunshine. It was not early for the cooks and stewards. They had risen at their usual hour, at work when all else was quiet. For once, the third mate would not be in for breakfast.

Facing the sun and with back to the town, east Stanley harbour was my destination, and I took an improvised route towards the shipwrecks that drew my attention. In a quiet backwater, two wooden hulks lay in slumped attitudes. They had certainly seen better times. Like a lectern over a fallen congregation, an information plaque stood on the tussocky ground above, and pronounced a potted history of the two vessels. Named *Golden Chance* and *Gentoo* they had been North Sea steam drifters from Lowestoft, brought south for a Falklands venture. A mile beyond lay a substantial wreck of a three-masted sailing ship, *Lady Elizabeth*. Her steel plates turned to rust, nestled beneath the arc of her prow, the distant red of *John Biscoe* spoke of a ship still vital and alive. It was a poignant depiction of harsh contrasts.

Lady Elizabeth had once been a vigorous creature of the elements, a demanding mistress for the attention of many crews. Now she lay as a grave to their endeavours. How many have served on *John Biscoe* in her thirty-five years and what will her fate be after this, her final voyage south? It was time to be back on the ship.

For the author, sketching ashore at Port Stanley provided a welcome break from shipboard duties. (Author's collection)

The jewelled stillness of morning was becoming ruffled. A distinct breeze ushered in from the north. Soon whitecaps patterned the harbour, and the wind cracked the flags. Tied up alongside, the orange-hulled supply ship *Typhoon* seemed aptly named. Later she was to transfer 200 tonnes of bunker fuel to *John Biscoe*, welcome ballast to set the ship deeper in the water. Through the narrows a freighter entered harbour to lie precariously at anchor in the gale, intimidatingly close to the vessels at her stern. A situation for general disquiet, she soon weighed anchor to move back into the wider expanse of Port William. On *Typhoon* the ship's dog barked, standing full-square and with nose high, defying the taunts of the wind.

Next to suffer this unruly element was *Falklands Protector*, which berthed with difficulty. In huge black letters, 'Fishery Patrol' dominated her flanks. She carried the burden of policing the extensive fisheries zone that encircles the islands.

A more local task was being attended to on our own decks. Cement had been mixed in an old bucket and small squares of canvas cut ready. It was a prudent measure to plug the drainage scuppers before taking fuel. Any accidental spillage into the harbour would have been a damaging and justly expensive crime. The seaman's skills are many. Expertly the trowel was applied around the canvas perimeter, securing a mat over the scupper holes which are studiously kept unblocked at sea.

The skills of the fourth engineer were also put on line as he controlled the distribution of fuel. It was an unseen task, as are so many that have their origins in the engine room, the mysterious power house and 'central hold' of the captain's respectful jesting. Pneumatic gauges indicated the content of each fuel tank. Relentlessly pumped aboard, valves were variously swung open and eased closed on time, in a manner to prevent ruptures to pipes or spillages. The bunkering agent stood by on deck as the chief engineer looked through round-rimmed spectacles at a sample bottle of fuel. A diplomatic firmness was needed to ensure delivery of the right quantity and quality of product. The delivery meter having been read by both parties at start and finish, a final figure was agreed and the paperwork exchanged. On deck the umbilical hose was uncoupled and the scuppers reopened. His duty done, in the engine room Roger cocked his hat and heaved a contented sigh.

I may have been off duty, but while aboard ship any are prone to be volunteered. With only a curtain drawn across the cabin door, I was easy prey. Thus the task of showing visitors around had fallen my way. It was a good question: 'How often is the crow's nest used?' 'Never,' was the reply. 'You'd freeze to death up there.' In a lofty position on the foremast, it added a touch of rugged romance to the ship's profile, yet had latterly served mainly as a platform for the searchlight and an unhelpful foil against the radar's forward-scanning pulses. There had been talk of removing it, but *John Biscoe* would never have been the same without her cute carbuncle.

On the bridge, navigation was explained in lay terms, but evidently still remained safe behind its veil of mystery. Later, the managers of the port were given a similar tour. Responding to my question about their knowledge on such matters, they answered that they were former Master Mariners, so knew nothing at all … Their downward gaze from the bridge into the ship's open cargo hold provided a window to the past. They were looking at a rare spectacle, a symbol of a dying tradition. In the era of the true general cargo ship such a scene would have been normal. Canvas tarpaulins rolled back, hatch beams and wooden hatch boards stacked on the side decks. Like a highway policeman's upraised arms, the two derricks were held aloft, directing the traffic of cargo between the ship and shore. At the two winches Colin and Tony drove their wire runners to the hand signals of the bosun. Meeting at a single hook in the rig, known as union purchase, their combination made light and rapid work of the boxed cargo of scientific equipment netted aboard.

Single-handed at the stern, a more modern crane was being operated, the gang of scientists hard-pressed to keep it supplied. On the quayside, opened containers were laboriously stripped of their contents by hand, or forklift driven enthusiastically by the chief officer. At the same time a duty Land Rover was aiding the escape of several off-duty staff. The little group had itchy feet and a mind to reach the summit of Mount Usborne, the high point of the islands. Suffering an enforced lack of exercise that befalls all who are captive aboard ship, the scrambling ascent confirmed their condition. Yet they eventually returned triumphant, with satisfied wind-tanned faces, but the careful gait betrayed weary limbs.

Going ashore was prompted by a range of desires: freedom to walk different paths; to drink a different ale; to telephone home; or fish from the quay, reeling in mullet on rods more used to northern trout. Already very much ashore, the desire for seagoing was not in Don's mind. He was more concerned with getting his bicycle fixed. Cycling the length of South America, and newly arrived in the Falklands, he was aware that *John Biscoe* was in Stanley. Old work connections had prompted him to try and visit the ship. His notional visit turned into a commitment of several months. For a moment he forgot about the bicycle that had stoically carried him over thousands of challenging miles. By word of mouth he had heard of a broadcast on Falklands Radio: *John Biscoe* had vacancies for crew. His

In safe hands, loading cargo with traditional derricks rigged for 'union purchase' was swift and sure. (Author's collection)

'Winged-out' cargo in the hold 'tween deck. (Author's collection)

Labour intensive: the paraphernalia and practice of securing the main cargo hatch. (Author's collection)

bicycle stowed carefully in the engine room, Don had secured a passage home to the UK by working as messman. He philosophically accepted this strange quirk of fate, only lamenting the prospect of the inevitable slow withering of muscles that hitherto had been honed to a peak of fitness by months of self-propelled travel.

* * *

The after deck was festooned with nets. Impressively clever in design, they posed basic problems of assembly. Encircling the black, fine-meshed heap, the unravellers pondered thoughtfully. Like a jellyfish out of its element it sprawled lifeless on the wooden deck. Only in the water would its graceful multiple form flourish, but by then beyond sight of admirers. In the previously empty laboratories, equipment of eye-catching complexity and unknown use emerged from packing cases, to be secured on benches. Home from home for the scientists, they established their domain in style.

Although humming with activity, an elemental calm still underpinned events. Everyone knew that soon *John Biscoe* would again depart for sea, but this time in a very different capacity than before.

In mid-afternoon the gangway was lifted, severing the link between two very different worlds. Clustered at the rails the scientists would feel it acutely. Beneath all our feet the life-pulse of the ship also beat with a growing strength, as she sped us towards the narrows and the sea. In the fine weather, good spirits prevailed, and the newly joined members of the company savoured the spectacle on deck. On either hand, the shores of Port William drew back. Ahead lay the open ocean and six weeks of work for the OBP – the Offshore Biological Programme.

Some eyes were more receptive to detail; soon it was spotted, striking awe into its admirers. For its hapless prey the peregrine falcon brought dread, and death on the wing. This was the fate for a thin-billed prion, a gentle seabird plucked in untimely fashion from the air and carried to an unlikely perch for preparation and consumption. On an aerial wire from the foremast the bird was coldly butchered. Severed off, the head fell to the deck. Retrieved by onlookers, it lay on the bench, a delicate beauty of bill and eye and soft grey plumage, ending obscenely in a torn carnage of staining red. The meal was insufficient. It took only a few minutes before the falcon returned. This time it chose the mainmast light upon which to sate its appetite, all the while aloof to the observers below. The prions did not die unremembered. Their fate was carefully recorded in the remarks

Kitted out for science; electronics are a vital component of the Offshore Biological Programme. (Author's collection)

pages of the all-embracing Met. Log. It had been a grave day for them, and the gloom was to spread by evening. As the bank of fog enveloped us, the bridge-wings became deserted of fair-weather friends.

Ocean science is a down-to-earth business. Gleaning the physical material is very much a practical art. Evolved over the years, the ship had been equipped for this role, temporarily assuming qualities and operational techniques akin to the world-ranging and dedicated oceanographic research ships that were my own area of expertise. At last I felt familiarly at home, particularly compared with those of my colleagues for whom the temporary evolution occurred but once a year.

Gear and equipment were resurrected, booms and outriggers were swung outboard, derricks and davits topped and guyed. There was a place for everything, and everything was in its place. Oddly sited pad-eyes and cleats that previously were foot snags for the unwary now grasped pulley blocks and ropes, their purpose made clear. Colin's remark was confident: 'There won't be a net before lunch.' I tended to agree. No sooner thought than the chief officer breezed in. 'They're ready!' Contradictions and the unexpected were to be normal.

It was a trial net, to check all was correct, and as a shakedown for the operators. It did not take long to discover the error. On the after deck, things were upside down. No excuse is needed for teasing, no minor event too trivial to attract mock scorn and jest. All were to become subject to this great leveller. The ship headed into the wind, at the required slow speed.

Routine recovery of the nets; pintado petrels were habitually in attendance. (Author's collection)

A night deployment of the RMT – Rectangular Mid-water Trawl. (Author's collection)

Deployed from an outrigger, the tow-fish controlled the actions of the trawl nets by acoustic signals. (Author's collection)

Hands waved and winches hummed as the multiple nets were laboriously lowered over the stern. Caught in the buoyant flow, the limp meshes streamed into shape, as a kite answers the pull of a lofty breeze. Held closed by a series of bars and wires, the nets each awaited the call to open on command, to capture samples at chosen depths, each discrete from its neighbour.

Hung from its own lengthy boom, the torpedo-shaped tow-fish communicated the acoustic signals. These opened and closed the mouths of the RMTs – the Rectangular Midwater Trawls. At each trailing end a collecting bag retained the catch. Hauls were not commercial, the contents hardly spectacular-looking. The prey was squid or krill, the vital minutiae in the food chain, and still elusive to our hunting.

Less so were the birds. The observers, too, were back with a vengeance. Theirs was to be an ordered discipline, the lee-side bridge-wing their workplace, binoculars the tools of their trade. With practised certainty, one of these scientists plunged into a bridge cupboard. The device he unearthed was a Husky. A clever but simple apparatus, it hooked neatly over the dodger. Computers can appear in unlikely places. Such was the Husky, programmed to record input of observations. In a plastic cover, the coded index was secured adjacent, listing the names of many species: dove prion, white-chinned petrel, macaroni penguin.

I took Mick to be a professional naturalist, such was the apparent ease with which he identified birds within the set compass of his observations. 'No, I'm a chemist, but I enjoy birdwatching more.' He pointed out the dark and darting black-bellied storm petrels, but declined to draw attention to the albatross. Its vast bulk spoke for itself. The extent of its extraordinary wanderings prompted heads to be shaken in disbelief. Breeding birds can fly thousands of miles before returning to their nests. Sustaining their growing chicks, immobile in youth, the young birds' down offers a natural protection from cold.

It is not so easy for humans, who take opportunities to scrounge if the prospect of acquiring garments comes their way. Opening the clothes locker door always induced such interest. As if by fatal attraction they appeared from nowhere. 'Oh, by the way, you wouldn't happen to have a spare pair of long socks, would you?'; 'Any chance of some thicker moleskins? – the wind whistles through these trousers.' Caught in a busy thoroughfare, the locker's position would have been the envy of a high-street outfitter. As stock keeper I can tell you that there was never a quiet time to visit the locker, with the ship and science running around the clock.

On a twelve-hour rota, scientists worked through the nights. A nocturnal routine operated, overlapping the four-hour periods of the ship's watches. This small army of intellectual workers also marched on their stomachs. The galley observed unusual hours as the cook prepared midnight meals. He appeared happy at his task, alone in his domain, which, on other occasions, was a swelter of coordinated activity, to meet the pressing expectations of daytime palettes. As reward, he reaped the luxury of an extra two-hour lie-in.

On the bridge, I was generously hailed the CTD-king of the North Sea. Over the years I had hove ships' bows to wind and maintained a manual dynamic position on many hundreds of occasions, to deploy this mainstay of ocean science that analyses sea conductivity, temperature and depth. At the end of its electrically transmitting wires, the delicate apparatus penetrated the water column from surface to seabed, continuously recording those parameters. Sampling bottles snapped closed at selected depths to bring up their individual contents intact, for further analysis on board.

From its own special side gantry the wire unwound from the storage winch, driven from the airy control position above. 'The only thing that works is the winch,' said Martin, the crewman operating the controls. He

Catches were meticuously sorted and logged. (Author's collection)

gestured dismissively at the panel, impressive-looking with gauges and counters, all resolutely registering zero. Meters always seem troublesome in the marine environment, a periodic headache for technicians. This system was a tenacious nuisance.

It was not alone in its idiosyncrasies. On the bridge, the bow thrusters, which helped keep the ship in position, were occasionally prone to creep and cut out; the echo sounder trace needed careful study to spot phantom depths. Beneath its monitor a book of correction tables lay open. The scientists would not be happy if their costly equipment had been driven into a seabed of lesser depth than indicated.

Keeping the wire vertical was a dynamic operation, belying the ship's apparent lack of motion. Wind and seas are far from constant, as are the vagaries of sub-surface currents, all of which can lead sub-marine apparatus astray. Taking over from the watch, I had been left with a wire angle that was 'good enough for Government work'. Shortly afterwards the wire, with qualities like a bandsaw, slewed suddenly beneath the ship.

Deployed by vertical conducting wire through the water column, measurements of conductivity, temperature and depth are relayed to the observing ship. Water samples are also remotely collected at discrete depths. (Author's collection)

This is a situation that, unchecked, has been known to penetrate the hulls of smaller wooden research vessels. Bringing the wind more on to the ship's side was the remedy: but for how long...? To those in cabins beneath, the sound was tiresome. The winch whined in wavering tones, like a bluebottle seeking escape from a closed room. There was no doubt when wire work was taking place.

***

The revelation came on 13 January. At dinner, Bob the third engineer had said he was going home from Stanley. He relayed it with a smile, as if somewhat relieved. Not wishing to pry, I stifled my question, intent on dealing with an unsettling feeling that had accompanied his announcement. Had the mention of home triggered a subtle envy? Was he not happy with the job? Like me, he was a relative newcomer, but of four months' standing. Was it the constraints of a long trip? No, after his leave he was to stand by *James Clark Ross*, the new ship being completed on Tyneside.

'Supper has just arrived.' The net was back aboard under the floodlights at Squid Station 1. Yet another meagre haul, but catching little tells as much as a bag of plenty. It was the dusk haul and in an hour the night tow would begin. A steam downwind at full speed filled the interim. Like a late Christmas decoration without an audience, the red-and-white all-round lights on the signal mast were switched off, removing the warm and rosy hue from the decks.

The course calculated, the helm was swung over and the engine control eased forwards. The lazy click of the compass hung in a moment of silent balance before its crazed gallop rattled in pursuit of the swinging ship. It was music to the watchkeeper's ears, painting signs of movement in an inky black night. The engines added their own voice. To see movement at first hand meant a glimpse over the side at the swelling marbled wake.

* * *

'The things I'll do for a pose,' mused Alan the electrical engineer. Parka-hooded and with a safety harness on, he appeared like a mountaineer determined to conquer those ill-disciplined control gauges on the deck equipment. Despite the half-glasses delicately balanced on his nose, his peerings at the lurid spaghetti of wiring had revealed nothing. It was time to look at the business end, high above the deck.

In the intense microcosm of life aboard ship, attention to detail was the lot of many in the daily round. Remote, and insignificant in the scale of the surroundings, far-off events also preyed on the mind. After dinner the radio listeners were silent, as the World Service spoke of Iraq and the deadline heralding punitive measures. Safe in our remoteness, the changing parochial fortunes of the crib players were a target for jests. Maurice was on a losing streak to Robin; the mealtime taunts of his colleagues were merciless.

My own regularity at meals was also a source for comment. The steward noted that my trim frame defied fattening. 'You're alright,' he said, 'you've got a metabolism.' Food was part of the wages; it was a good way of boosting earnings. 'The amount John eats, he must be on fifty grand a year!' Munching on breakfast toast and marmalade allowed for absent staring out of a distant window. The horizon rose and dipped like an uncertain thermometer, but less mesmerising glimpses stimulated the imagination and sense of mischief. All of a sudden the window was completely blocked by a magnificent presence. It seemed as if a Sunderland flying boat had materialised from history, to fly at our side. In reality it was a wandering albatross, patrolling in our updraughts. Minutes later a dangling rope

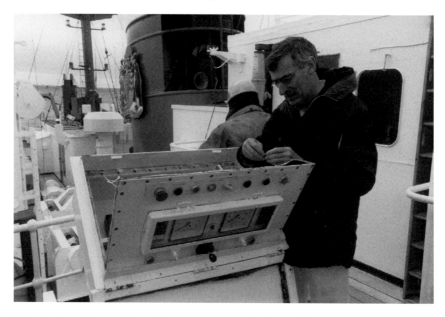

Electrical engineer Alan Jones traces a fault in the control box of the hydrographic davit. (Author's collection)

swung back and forth across the pane, hoisting up a small rubber bucket. The sea temperature was being taken. Maurice and I hatched a plan to lie in wait beneath, in the concealment of the shelter deck and fill the passing receptacle with water from the steamer. 'Chief, the sea is boiling!'

Squid Station 1 had yielded up its secrets. It was time for pastures new. The tightly packed programme list began to acquire red ticks as the allotted tasks were completed. It was the nearest we ever allowed ourselves to crossing off the days. The passage to South Georgia was a two-day run. These islands are more than just another group. The name is synonymous with heroic drama, exploit, half-remembered tales and first-strike for a notable international conflict. *John Biscoe* was to spend several weeks in its vicinity and intimacy, and be touched by its grand wilderness.

Our course loosely followed the North Scotia Ridge in its wide submarine arc. The only pimples of rock to rear up from its expansive sweep surfaced 150 miles west of South Georgia. Dots on the chart, they nevertheless demanded attention. Too often had they been passed in the distance, as suggestions on the horizon or a blip on the radar. Shag Rocks thrust 200 feet above the waves. The crown of its neighbour would gash the surface into a seething turmoil of white. Black Rocks by name, theirs was the greater lurking danger. John, the cautious navigator, joked, 'As they're rocks in the middle of the ocean, you tend to avoid them like the plague, not go between them!' However, that was our intention: research ships often confound the general rule.

'It will be a good "tick",' he continued, the slang for a memorable event. He would already have paced the dividers across the chart and realised the pleasure would eventually befall his watch, in the small hours of morning. Being 9 miles apart, these rock islets were like the ruined pillars of a mighty gateway. Our course lay between them, and here was the unknown, another opportunity to obtain depths. In the watch preceding, observers could see the gradual rise from the deep towards the shelf. At midnight the first tentative echo appeared on radar. Our distance and bearing coincided with the 500-fathom line; all of these were points for reassurance in the careful scrutiny of our position. 'If you are happy, John, I'll wander down.' 'Delirious' was his reply, a parting shot for having left him an interesting watch. My own view of those rocks was limited to that one radar image. Nets were towed overnight in their northern proximity before resuming passage to South Georgia.

Serenely alone in our travels, it was a day for reflection and chores. With long sight, some gazed knowingly at the sky, while others addressed the tedium of stock taking. Our erstwhile long-distance cyclist had settled in to his temporary role as messman. Previously involved in meteorology for the Survey, Don was a fan of the fresh air. He emerged from below decks intent on nostalgia. Reverently he turned the pages of hand-printed code numbers in the current book of weather observations. 'There was a time I knew all the codes,' he said with quiet pride. We discussed the minor traumas of trying to assess the types of clouds present, or the size and period of swell waves. Our agonies were coincident, which for me, as an amateur, was reassuring.

The task of taking stock of stores fell to the chief officer and bosun. In the cabin they sat on the carpet, surrounded by an explosion of small stores. Taken from the goldmine known as the mate's locker, there was a hardware shop in miniature scattered between them. 'This is no time to be playing with your Meccano sets,' was the witticism which fell on unappreciative ears. Over the months many inventories were to be made in the run-up to the vessel's final docking. There was much to be accounted for, the accumulation of many years, to be distributed who knew where, on the sad day when the Ship-for-Sale sign would be raised.

My first inkling of South Georgia was casually caught from a forward window as the bow dipped low. The sight brought an instantaneous thrill. New land, and with it a personal sense of discovery, diluted by the easy recognition of others: 'Oh, there's South G.' An island fully 90 miles in length, our landfall was made at its small western outliers of Main, Trinity and Bird islands. On the last, another permanent British base is situated.

We began our search 10 miles to the north. Finding krill was never going to be easy. In the daylight hours they swarm together but at dusk, like sardine shoals, they disperse so widely as to be undetectable by the sonar. Its regular pulse rang out like the sound of a tennis champion's serve, and was not returned, marking time into the dark hours and the neon glow of a bridge where night-sight is jealously guarded.

The searchlight neither swept nor pulsed. It knew its task and was of fixed intent, directing its attention unswervingly forward. Nestled in the high vantage of the crow's nest, it was routinely used and was to prove its worth. The tight beam silhouetted the foremast into sharp-edged blackness, angled downwards like a virtual forestay to brace its tall pedestal. It looked disconcertingly vertical until viewed from either bridge-wing. Flung far ahead, on clear nights it reflected up weakly, an optical rebound into the sky. It drew the eye expectantly to its illumined spot, a vacant stage awaiting a variety of performances. The ghostly flickering of white wings was plucked from out of the dark obscurity, birds like shy schoolchildren, daring the limelight before a hasty retreat. Wave crests startled in their impersonation of ice, assured of an audience until their trickery was revealed. In storms, the onrushing parades of seas were marbled to a bright turmoil of white and green, as the light plunged then reared skyward, in unison with the ship's motion. In calms, the light competed with snowflakes dancing in swirling eddies. True snow additionally cast a pale halo while fog further softened its penetration into the void, to bathe the ship in patterns of eerie shadow.

Sounds also added their riches. A haunting Irish melody played softly below emanated from the chief engineer's penny whistle. The unusual strains of a foreign voice across the ether called to *John Biscoe*. It was not an entire surprise; another vessel had been detected in the area. *Damien II* was a remarkable boat, designed by her owner for cruising in Antarctic waters. A steel-hulled yacht, her hollow keel carried fuel, yet was retractable, allowing her sleek form to be beached at need. As old friends, her owner and Captain Elliott spoke on the radio. Going below in the darkness, his smile was felt if not seen, as he recalled a connection spanning the previous two decades.

* * *

A light had suddenly appeared in a vaguely familiar room. This resolved into my cabin, viewed across the token restraining leeboard of the bunk. The echo of the steward's voice percolated slowly into my awaking consciousness as he closed the door behind him. He had relayed a message, something about an inflatable boat, and eight o'clock. Feeling like a beached seal I was reluctant to move. My response was unenthusiastic, but

A fixed and reassuring light probes the mysterious darkness ahead. (Author's collection)

the window curtains did it again. The revealed spectacle was an inspiring amphitheatre of extremes. I discovered how much I had missed the colour green. Its hue personified tranquillity in the mellow morning light. Close before me lay Grass Island. Frequently changing, the ship's flexible programme had caught me on the hop. An overnight decision had brought *John Biscoe* on a mystery tour for the majority who were about to wake. We were all glad to be there.

To be told we were in Leith harbour brought a delightful confusion. There was no resemblance to its northern namesake, no city of Edinburgh within commuting distance. The cluttered village of grey and rusting corrugated metal was testimony to a significant former occupancy. Dwarfed within the bowl of the embracing mountains, the old whaling station drew our attention. To one side lay the enduring symbols of a graveyard. Bone-white goalposts were defiant edifices of man's recreations.

These finer points were discovered later; the moment demanded more immediate measures. Two anchor cables stretched out from the ship's bows. Beyond the stern a huge mooring buoy sat incongruous in its bright pristine coat of painted yellow. The boat was needed to carry the ends of two ropes for attachment to its copious metal ring. Snaking bights once more trailed in the water as the wind blew them sideways. Clambering on to the buoy's substantial steps, the weighty mooring shackles were lugged out of the boat. Wielding the long metal spike, the securing pins were tightened. Twirling a raised hand in gesture towards the ship, the signal was acknowledged. The ropes were hauled taut, to a matching tension. Similar careful treatment with the anchors left the ship in a firm unmoving grip against the mischievous gusts that bowled down the surrounding hill slopes. It was a necessary constraint so that the scientists could calibrate their fish-finding echo sounders.

Around the summits of the higher mountains, the streamers of clouds flew in a more regular breeze, smoothing their grand summits. Larssen Peak reached beyond 5,000 feet, one of several in a lofty and snow-covered arc. With possessive pride the doctor smoothed out his map of South Georgia. Obtained from the shelves of its famous London publishers, he carried others with him, items of both function and beauty.

Leith harbour appeared a tiny inlet in the scale of the whole island, a measure to impress its true size and grandeur. Slowly the mountains became veiled, as a soft, draping rain settled in, dimpling the water and glossing all surfaces with a liquid sheen. 'You'll get a wet behind wearing those' was a remark I came to agree with, and I returned to exchange the baggy Ventile windproofs for more suitable attire. The chief officer and I were off ashore on an unusual errand to an unusual location.

It was called Catcher Pier. In its heyday, the whale hunters would have secured to this substantial jetty. On that particular day a less threatening and more modern vessel lay quietly alongside. The large white yacht flew the German flag, limp in the stillness. On the pier end, neat parcels of

Trainee seaman David Miles helps secure stern ropes to a mooring buoy in Leith harbour. (Author's collection)

timber gave evidence of recent effort. This 'small amount of timber' shrank and grew depending upon who viewed it. To its owner it was a handy-sized 1-ton consignment. To the chief officer, charged with having it lifted and stowed on board *John Biscoe*, it appeared less handy. The tape measure was drawn out repeatedly to gauge the bundles. Lengths of 20 feet stretched near to the size of the ship's hatch opening.

It was a matter of depth that found us paddling off the pier, probing through the kelp with the lead-line. A total of 5 fathoms reducing to 3 was an acceptable clearance for the ship to berth her bows alongside on a future visit to collect the timber. No sign of the wreck could be detected; it was charted as lying in the same spot, although the aura of its potential threat lingered beneath the waving weedy fronds.

The dampening veil drew back to leave a welcome freshness. In a shallow arc a rainbow hung above the entrance to the bay, terminating at the yellow buoy which lay as a crock of gold in the afternoon sun. On steep flanking slopes the bare wet rock shone between scree and snow, as wisps of drying vapours hung in the air. It was a fitting performance from the island as *John Biscoe* left to resume her work. A return to this part of South Georgia in early February was eagerly anticipated. It would mark the midpoint in the relentless round of sampling and analysis of catches that was the crux of the Offshore Biological Programme.

February had arrived: 'South Georgia at its magnificent best!' Captain Elliott should know, and his statement of fact did not disguise the thrill of such a glorious spectacle. Our own silence supported his enthusiasm. Once more the lifting fog played its part in ensuring the drama of our mid-afternoon arrival in Stromness Bay. Outstretching from its copious palm, three stubby fingers indented the coast: the harbours of Leith, Stromness and Husvik. At the tip of each, the former whaling stations bore the same names. Split by the headland of Harbour Point our approach allowed a tantalising glimpse into Stromness, otherwise hidden by the verdant sentinel of Grass Island.

The spectators were free of care. Not so the chief officer, whose watch it befell to make our safe entrance. Black Rocks were the guide, and a careful index of distance ensured our passage between them and that of Middle Ground Rock. A bold swing to the west on to the heading of Harbour Point then brought us through dangers into the confines of Leith Harbour. 'You're not cutting the corner, Chris?' exclaimed Robin. 'Who, me?' responded the captain dryly, as with local knowledge he followed his own visual marks.

We expected to have company and even assistance in our intended manoeuvres. The bright thread of a boat's wake confirmed the presence of others. Her parent ship hove into view, a rare sight in these unfrequented waters. In livery of black and buff, the RMAS *Throsk* was busy in her own

Royal Maritime Auxiliary
Service *Throsk* carried out
environmental protection
work at the former
whaling station. (Author's
collection)

movements, canopied by a pall of blue vapour that hung lazily over her
labours. Her worthy task was to help clean up the whaling station beyond,
and render it environmentally safe. At Catcher Pier she had already tested
the water, laying the ghost of the wreck which had niggled in the mind.
So the jetty did offer a safe if cramped berth. In mellow English tones her
captain intimated his findings. Mooring themselves to the buoy of our own
earlier occupancy, the way was clear for us to berth at the pier end.

Hovering mid-harbour and with press-ganged volunteers of scientists,
the launch was lowered and sent shoreward to take our ropes. The bow
thrusters would have been very useful, yet here was no place for its
directing jet of water, the dense fronds of kelp a perfect blockage to the
suction demands of the intake. A mechanical tantrum provided a diversion
to add to the trials of the moment.

Clutching the end of an offending hydraulic pipe, the chief engineer
stood with fingers quenching the upwelling oil. The winch had sprung a
leak in its efforts to haul in the stern ropes. The dustpan coped valiantly,

an efficient scoop to remove the sluicing tide of dark liquid from off the wooden deck. In the aftermath, David agreed that he always got the best jobs, sweeping up the sticky carpet of sawdust with a smile. Like the first threads of a spider's web in a forgotten corner, the ship's ropes clung to the rusty shore bollards. Half of the ship protruded beyond the pier end, the propeller safe in deep and uncluttered waters.

Gangways are often a bind. Ensuring a safe connection between ship and shore often taxes creative talents, when overcoming the shortfalls of facilities and the vagaries of changing tides. It is a sensible and legal requirement to come and go by proper gangway, but temptation often lingers on small ships to take a shortcut – just this once. The gangway of *Throsk* lay waiting on the jetty. Its end lifted on top of the well deck rails, a cumbersome cross-stitch of ropes held it in place. Ending ominously close to the other side of the pier, a commandeered gas bottle was pressed to serve as a blocking bollard, to prevent an untimely and undignified plunge. Strung beneath, the safety net seemed unnecessary as it gently brushed the iron-clad walkway.

Eager explorers watched the erecting of this, their pathway to exploration. They had entered their names into the Shore Walks Book, as well as the time of departure, the intended destination and the time of return. Hands irritably fanned the air to wave away the unexpected and unwelcome flies. Beneath the surface two divers plaited their uncoiling bubbles as they explored the kelp forests.

A cordial invitation to share in the ship's next meal was extended to the captain of *Throsk*. In close proximity the two vessels were yet divided by different time zones; our clocks ticked an hour behind theirs. Dinner had already come and gone, and, with a sated satisfaction, thanks and a decline were returned. *Throsk* had acted as an impromptu mail ship from Stanley. Collected by our launch it was an impressive bonus, and a pleasure to distribute the coloured envelopes to their surprised recipients.

An unsettling rumour had been rife: the prospect of an extended voyage. Reactions to it were mixed: shrugs of indifference, sinking disappointment, a just agitation or suppressed pleasure. The source of this confusion lay in a distant and dramatic region, held in the ice-clutch of the southern Weddell Sea. Around the wardroom table, in dark-clad formality and relaxed attitudes, chairs were pushed back.

Following the meal, the rumours were made official. The rule in the Antarctic secures mutual aid across all borders and asks for no reparation. Specialist ships from different nations make the region their operating territory, and in its harsh extremity can feel cocooned by this knowledge of unstinting potential assistance. Within the British Antarctic Survey no

Cautiously approaching Catcher Pier. (Author's collection)

All quiet at Catcher Pier. (Author's collection)

less is expected. Its other vessel, *Bransfield*, had suffered a major setback. Working pack ice towards Halley base, the southernmost British presence on the continent, a burnt-out armature had cut her power by half, and with it reduced her speed and capacity to work in ice. The yoke of her remaining work for the current season seemed about to be placed on to the mature shoulders of *John Biscoe*. In distant places her fate was being mapped out.

On the ship a different map was being regarded. It had been drawn in 1979 and had seen much care in its making. The penned lines and neat labels accurately depicted the complexity of the Leith whaling station when in operation. Each building would have seen a life of its own, beyond the terse descriptions; 'E' Barrack, Swedish hut, piggery, coppersmith, blubber cookery, guano factory, hens. The list seemed endless, defying the imagination to conjure scenes of their daily functioning.

On Catcher Pier, bulky machinery lay rusting. The third engineer voiced his recognition as if glimpsing old and familiar friends: a horizontal borer, a vertical milling machine, a centre lathe. The fourth engineer peered into the gloom of an isolated shed and likewise exclaimed, 'The last time I saw steam reciprocating gear like that was in the sixties.'

Our evening explorations wandered like a butterfly's flight, bizarre sights guiding our feet to left and right. What lay behind the green door of the Swedish hut? I did not expect to see a full-size snooker table, naked of its felt covering, the slate cracked and defaced by graffiti. Touched by the breeze that eddied through the shattered windows, the net pockets quivered as if in memory of potted blacks.

Off the long hospital corridors the door-less rooms were a litter of senile decay: broken beds, scattered mattresses, the bathroom sinks deluded in their capacity to cleanse. Nearby, the tiny cemetery was bordered by a low white-painted fence, an albino apparition in the drabness of the dusk. In the ensuing dark the night-watchman leaned at the rails in contemplation. The dull images of sheds were pale shapes in the ship's lights. Small waves tolled on the unseen shore and gently nudged the launch at her overnight mooring. The ship responded to a greater surge, echoed by dubious sounds from the yielding tyre fenders.

I Dag Alt Er Mulig..., 'Today All Is Possible...' It was a Norwegian book title for personal inspiration, spotted by casual chance from an unlikely source. That the whaling station library remained largely intact seemed an enigma. As a jewel within the carnage, the little room held fast its brittle store of knowledge, fact and fiction. The neatly stacked shelves of books appeared to wait for a revival, patient of the chafing winds that scoured the green-painted room. The musty smell was subtle, the sight of an empty gin bottle less so. English and Norwegian books abounded. The serendipity that directed my gaze to a title I could translate gave satisfaction; my spare-time labours of learning Norwegian were not entirely wasted. Cared for by occasional visiting ships, the library defied desecration. It was a meaningful symbol of something precious. Temptation to remove a choice souvenir seemed largely to have been resisted. The same could not be said for the tins of Brasso. The ship's engine-room stocks were depleted, so it was with a shining countenance that the donkeyman proclaimed this most welcome find. On a caterpillar track, rusted beyond redemption, the gleaned tins stood to purposeful attention.

The time had come for loading timber. The heavy wooden hatch boards and beams were laboriously removed, revealing the shallow 'tween deck. Its false floor of boards was opened up in like fashion by the grapples of gloved hands and hook, to reveal the more substantial depths of the lower hold for inspection. A family of large wooden containers clustered together companionably, each containing a rough terrain buggy. On each container, carefully stencilled figures denoted their details. The code number, overall dimensions and 'cube', together with gross weight, were the only marks on the otherwise plain packages. To accommodate the stock of timber, they had to be moved sideways from the centre of the hold, 'winged-out' and stacked beneath the deck above.

Ingenuity was the key to overcoming such an awkward move. Lengthy webbing strops were unrolled and secured about the angular girth of each load. Hooked and hanging on the end of the long hoist, in turn they

Skilled hands make light work of loading the timber, which eventually filled the hold to within an inch. (Author's collection)

became pendulous weights of potent force. Their sharp-edged bulk could crush unwary fingers, and splinter ribs with ease. At the perimeter of skylight above, by the hatch coaming on deck, the bosun directed the crew working the winches. His hand movements responded to his overview and the clipped instructions emanating from beneath. Timing and coordination again played their part, as, with a man-made momentum, the boxes were swung towards their new place of rest. A shouted 'come back!' sent the hook plunging, allowing the load to land heavily and quell its potential to cause damage. Hefty levers and the sweated brow eventually left the intended space clear. The hold would become closely stowed to within a lucky inch of being brimful. The last of the long bundles were loaded into the 'tween deck. Unlike their fellows beneath, these would need proper lashing. Long chains were riven through holes overhead, tediously wrapped about the cargo and led aloft once more. Ratchets were attached to tighten the chains. Within their grasp the timber was held immovable.

If the visit to Leith harbour was a mid-programme break for the scientists, it was no less so for the crew. With half a day spent on cargo work, the remaining free hours were jealously coveted. Some walkers had risen at four o'clock in the morning, leaving early for the trek to Stromness and its own whaling station. They saw the changes in the day, the cycle from a damp dawn and a growing diffuse light, to the rising and breaking of cloud and the appearance of the sun.

CHAPTER 5

The *John Biscoe* Delivers All...

John Biscoe: the toast of Port Stanley – a notable trans-shipment – King George Island – field station recovery – Deception Island – a passage of superlatives – Faraday – farewell from Signy – Grytviken – Husvik – Bird Island – St Patrick's Day – brimful once more.

'In case anybody is interested, there are a couple of whales ahead.' The disembodied voice of the second officer floated through the wardroom on the public address system, interrupting talk of the moment. All was to be forgotten, thanks to the two creatures which by lucky chance had crossed our path. Hardened observers, dulled by many more-distant sightings, did not sit down from the windows but rushed forth, leaving meals to grow cold at the table. Infection was spreading fast, as it always does from such a close meeting.

The two southern right whales were treated as special envoys. The ship was stopped dead, to float quietly in waiting. The aura of their presence beside us instilled a calm that washed over the whole company. Nothing had so instantly united the ship. As the decks became crowded, it seemed that this moment was the most significant. The most valuable 'science' of the voyage was being shared in common by everyone.

It was truly a time for awe and reverence, not at the frigid grandeur of icebergs or the threat of southern storm, but of Life and Mystery. In our common eagerness, what were we so innocently acknowledging? Perhaps something deep in us, sensitivity buried, and thought lost beneath the complexities of modern living. Touched, or rediscovered, there was spontaneous celebration, nothing short of a quiet, irrepressible joy.

At home in the Antarctic: RSS *John Biscoe* moored in the Meek Channel, at Faraday scientific base. (Author's collection)

British Antarctic Survey's Base F – Faraday – on Galindez Island off the west coast of the Antarctic Peninsula. Its main function was the study of geophysics, meteorology and ionospherics. (Author's collection)

Funnel crest: The National Arms of the Falkland Island Dependencies. The motto 'Research and Discovery' reflects the aims of the British Antarctic Survey. (Author's collection)

John Biscoe at her registered home of Port Stanley, in the Falkland Islands. (Author's collection)

Top and middle: A delicate and demanding business: Captain Chris Elliott cons the ship in difficult ice conditions. (Author's collection)

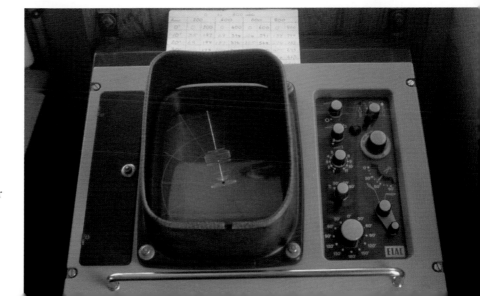

The pinging sonar gives early audible and visual warning of hidden underwater navigational dangers ahead. (Author's collection)

Hydrographic surveying: the chief officer, Robin Plumley, painstakingly creates a new line of depth soundings for dispatch to the makers of Admiralty charts, to improve safety of navigation for all, in areas where accurate data is scarce or non-existent. (Author's collection)

Fair-weather jobs en route for the Antarctic: 'blacking down the stays', covering the ship's steel standing with a traditional protective coating. (Author's collection)

Off-duty chores: the second officer, John Harper, enjoys a spot of ironing. (Author's collection)

Serving up a feast: the galley staff dish out the eagerly awaited Christmas lunch. (Author's collection)

Christmas lunch is much enjoyed in the officers' wardroom... (Author's collection)

...and by the scientific and support staff in the FIDs' mess room. (Author's collection)

As a designated Meteorological Observing Vessel, a meticulous record was maintained with observations every six hours, for coding and onward radio transmission to BAS bases and the UK Met Office. Principal Observing Officer Trevor Boult carried out regular maintenance of the weather station's Stevenson's screens. (Author's collection)

During the Offshore Biological Programme, intensive observations of wildlife were logged on to a dedicated data recorder. (Author's collection)

For the duty lookout, ice creates an extra dimension, especially in poor visibility. (Author's collection)

Fog brings an extra chill to the polar navigator's day. (Author's collection)

Bergy bits drifting in the current of the Meek Channel brought added complications to the ship, moored close to Faraday base. (Author's collection)

At Port Stanley, loading logistical and lifeline equipment and stores for the scientific bases. (Author's collection)

Loaded cargo snug in the 'tween deck. (Author's collection)

Messing about with boats. Responsible for the daily care of the four inflatable boats, the author attends to fuelling matters. (Author's collection)

Leith Harbour, Stromness Bay, South Georgia: a dramatic location for a former whaling station operated by Christian Salvesen. As part of a clean-up operation, *John Biscoe* loaded a consignment of dressed timber for removal to the Falklands. (Author's collection)

Near the end of the newly built runway at Rothera base, *John Biscoe* inaugurates the jetty named in her honour. (Author's collection)

Protecting the environment: removal of segregated wastes from Rothera for further processing at the Falklands. (Author's collection)

Time to leave: as the Antarctic autumn creeps in, the sea tentatively begins to freeze again. (Author's collection)

Off Port Stanley, the governor's launch conveys the official party to attend the farewell function aboard *John Biscoe*. (Author's collection)

Farewell: an eleven-gun salute is fired as *John Biscoe* takes her final leave of Port Stanley. (Author's collection)

Above and opposite top: The Antarctic at its mesmerising best. (Author's collection)

A pristine parting gift from the Antarctic. (Author's collection)

John Biscoe's new-build replacement, RRS *James Clark Ross*. In her own davits, carried aboard with pride, is the former workboat tug of the *John Biscoe*. (Photo by Swan Hunters)

The author. (Author's collection)

On South Georgia, wildlife displayed passing interest or total disregard of human visitors. (Author's collection)

Above: Moonscape across the Argentine islands to the Antarctic Peninsula. (Author's collection)

Left: At Rothera base, huskies provided pulling power and canine companionship. (Author's collection)

A memorable meeting with southern right whales. (Author's collection)

Beneath the very bows, in close company, the whales glided in a shimmering suspension of slow movement. Their ethereal images played tricks with the eyes, dissolving and swelling as they undulated in the sky of their own world. Here, our two worlds coincided. A mottled, blunt and calloused nose rose to the surface, and reared beyond; a smooth expanse of back followed, a great expulsion of breath sent plumed vapours to blow a fleeting rainbow in the air. A lazy fluke flopped and waved, slipping from sight in a gentle liquid welter. As they passed repeatedly from side to side, playing a slow-motion game, the captivated audience rippled across the cluttered decks in pursuit. Cameras ran dry of film. 'Now's the time to put the price up'; 'Walk round with an usherette's tray and you'll make a fortune.'

As we reluctantly resumed our passage back to the Falkland Islands, none would forget this rendezvous. We had glimpsed individuals at close hand, a meeting within the scale of our humanity. Some eyes would have been raised to the snow-clad mountains of South Georgia receding over the horizon, recalling Leith harbour with confusion, and the rusting remnant symbol of very different meetings: the clamour and horror from the heyday of whaling.

Called at a dawn of grey and wet gloom, the mantle of friendly forgetful sleep evaporated. Once more back in Stanley, it was an early start, and unspoken questions hung in the air. Yet it was to be a propitious move and none too soon. The wind that frequently rose mid-morning was to keep to form; its untimely attentions were most unwelcome. Close by, a sombre vessel lay at anchor, black and lifeless save for the wan glimmer of a single light. *John Biscoe* was soon to secure to her side and discharge the timber brought from South Georgia. Abandoned by Argentinians and left to a neglected fate, this craft had since found a local benefactor to resurrect her to a new and useful role. From the treasure house of inspired names, she had become known as *Black Pig*.

Her flanks were neither yielding nor welcoming. The skin was angular and solid. Despite a careful and gentle approach, our first contact was damaging. The stowed work platform acted as a buffer and buckled on impact, one more cost to the carriage of the good-turn cargo. In comparison to its loading, the discharge of the timber was swift. Slyly the wind had risen during the peak of activity, swinging the two ships' combined bulk and testing *Black Pig*'s anchor cable. Bar taut, it held against dragging or parting. Parting company from this platform was easy, the sole favour gleaned from the wind, demanding only coordination in swiftly letting go the ropes. Soon the ship was secure at her usual quayside berth. The trip was over, yet in the following days she needed moving on three occasions.

Pausing in her role as a creature of the ocean, *John Biscoe* accepted the periodic upheaval of intense activity which emptied her. Cabins, laboratories, hold and deck spaces became like a vacuum, urgent for refilling. Though empty, they still echoed with the voices of long and persevering occupancy. The hold offered vacant possession. On the quayside in containers, and within the cavernous sheds, the fresh cargo awaited attention. It would be augmented by products still deep in the stows of *Bransfield*, making her slow way northwards towards Stanley.

Two small keys fell into my outstretched hand and two cargo sheets were grasped. Clutching all, I went ashore in search of our cargo. Finding the two red containers took some time; they were not where I had been told. In puzzlement the strange identification numbers were compared; those before me bore no resemblance. They materialised at a distance from the ship, tucked out of sight. With relief, the numbers agreed.

Behind the sealed doors the boxed cargo would also tally, but their packing had been ill-conceived. All would soon be revealed when the doors were swung open. Sounds of disbelief greeted the sight of the contents. The containers had been packed back-to-front. The first hefty containers were labelled for Rothera base, yet the immediate cargo to be loaded was for Faraday and Signy. This all lay beyond reach. Such an error onboard ship would be more than just frowned upon. Un-stuffing the containers was burdensome, an extra tedium in the already busy schedule.

Job descriptions were set aside in the press of events. Ship's staff acted as stevedores; the mates were joined by the radio officer to strop the slings about the cargo packages and tally their transfer aboard. In the morning he had been perched precariously atop the radar mast, not for the first time effecting an airy repair to the scanner aerial. Ever circling, these slowly revolving rotors maintained a relentless rhythm in their vigilance. Unseen in their high elevation, their rotating shadows were cast onto decks and masts. Stopped on arrival in port, their rest was only to be short.

'I think he knows the way' was the comment as I visually checked the radar scanner before bringing it back to life. A distant memory prompted my reply: 'I've been caught out before by a captain who wanted a radar distance.' It was not to be a lengthy voyage. The Falkland Islands Company jetty could be clearly seen less than 2 miles distant. Over many years, during her visits to Stanley, *John Biscoe* had secured to this convenient quay. The move back for the duration was another homecoming, significant to old hands. Inevitably they concluded that it would be for the very last time. In answer to such nostalgic vein, the farewell dance had been conceived. The town hall booked, the invitations issued, it was fitting for the ship to assume her former berth, to become once again part of the waterfront landscape of Stanley.

Recently arrived in the harbour anchorage, another vessel added a latter-day and seasonal view. *Fuki Maru 63* was a Japanese fishing boat, a squid-jigger by trade. Her deck-line festooned with a forest of tall, latticed posts, each bore a powerful light used to lure prey. Tempted ashore, her crew chattered in good-natured groups, gaudy in multicoloured garb.

Within the town hall the walls were being decorated with the bright bunting of our ship's signal flags. Seconded from the bridge-wing locker, their unique patterns added a nautical colouring to the interior. The Survey's Land Rover was kept busy in transferring kegged beer and food; the event would be attended by hundreds.

'Are we going in mufti, or uniform?' was the detailed query. The response to the notion of uniform was swift: 'It's a dud idea!' Seemingly at odds with this consensus, I found myself thus dressed in the early evening as a decorous precaution. Distinguished visitors were potentially to arrive, and it was fitting that they be greeted formally. Keeping a comfortable weather eye on the quay from the wardroom, it was coincidence that a year-old newspaper carried an article about one particular guest. Leafing absently through *Penguin News*, the voice of the Falklands, the profile of the Governor of the Falkland Islands presented itself. The photograph would assure recognition. Close to hand the governor's standard was ready to be hoisted.

A red Range Rover was an unusual limousine, but functional for the islands' terrain. Escorted by the chauffeur, the governor's wife graced the ship in his absence. Resplendent in pale shimmering suits, the captain and chief officer hosted as diplomatic executives.

Aboard ship the calm was as profound as the party ashore was vibrant. In the acts of socialising, the revellers responded to group activity, extrovert in their enjoyment. To individual tastes, those caretaking the ship could indulge in an uncompromising fancy. The acoustics of the wardroom were found pleasing because of its vacant stillness, responsive to the strains of the penny whistle in its repertoire of reels, laments and jigs. In the back of the mind lurked the prospect of problems with the return of the partygoers. Gangways and steep steps can appear deceiving to potentially double-vision eyes. The electrician and I looked at the well-illuminated gangway, with its additional lights, with satisfaction. We agreed that at least we had done our part. Both of us had individual memories of long-past injuries related to the good-time-induced misuse of ships' gangways. It was a pleasant surprise next morning that I had not been called out of my bunk in the small hours. In darkened cabins, for a few the hour of rising would have come too soon. Perversely, the headache would confirm a good time. Antics or excesses would be discussed at length, a source for further amusement, or the shaking of disbelieving heads.

Morning stillness cosseted the harbour. On the public jetty, an old London taxi cast its dark reflection on the still water, adding to the colourful inverted image of the ship and wooden warehouses. Even to a fresh eye, *John Biscoe* seemed completely at home. Alongside the modern floating jetty further east, the imposing presence of *Bransfield* also seemed properly placed. She had arrived a few hours previously, the traumas of her most recent voyage thankfully behind her. They were to be raised often in the safe comfort of harbour tales.

Received aboard earlier, the ashes of a notable Antarctic traveller were taken into care. It was to be *John Biscoe*'s privilege to carry, and Captain Elliott's to scatter, the remains of Group Captain J. H. Lewis, for his widow and family. As a final resting place, the remote and unique grandeur of Deception Island was the chosen ground.

* * *

The thin wires of the radio aerials were not often lowered, but it was a detail best not overlooked. Taut and seemingly delicate, they stretched almost invisibly between the masts. They were no match for the hefty wire of *Bransfield*'s forward crane, kept tight not by a hand-hauled rope, but by a 1-ton metal ball. This crane was eventually to trans-ship *Bransfield*'s cargo to *John Biscoe*. The radio aerials were removed and the derricks slewed outboard to allow free scope for the cargo operations.

Berthing close astern of *Bransfield* was another occasion. High vantage points were filled on both ships to witness this rare meeting in a southern port. We were in no doubt that *John Biscoe* stole the show.

Also recently delivered aboard was a video of the launch of *James Clark Ross*, which was shown to an audience with a complexity of feelings and interests. As the eventual replacement for *John Biscoe*, it was very evident that she was worlds apart in size and appearance. Her awesome capability and technology represented the concepts and ideals of the next century. Yet, in her compactness and simplicity, *John Biscoe* had worked many wonders, and in the extended voyage to come would deliver everything that was asked of her.

With the time-honoured words spoken by Her Majesty the Queen – 'May God bless all who sail in her' – a tense pause followed the shattering champagne, before the new vessel gained a speedy momentum. A raucous orchestra of sirens and tugs' whistles welcomed the new arrival to her buoyant home. On the Harbourmaster's launch I had had my own privileged viewpoint on the historic occasion, to see her test the Tyne waters of my own home port. At the current moment *James Clark Ross* would still be having her newly created and empty spaces fleshed out into a living ship.

The hold and afterdeck of *John Biscoe* awaited the day's cargo. The first was propelled along the quay. A consignment of petrol disgorged from *Bransfield* was rolled in ragged and noisy convoy, brought to rest in an ever spreading pool of drums. Slung aboard in pairs, muscle-power stowed them in their tight nest at the stern. The forklift driver enjoyed the rain. Enclosed within the glass canopy he revelled in the metal quay, turned to a skating rink by the downpours. Wheels span round to gain grip, and skidding manoeuvres were made in reverse, bringing the crates within reach of the lifting hook. With careful admiration the stevedoring crew stood at a discreet distance. Activity was feverish. Approaching lunchtime, a heartfelt comment was made: 'I still haven't phoned my bloody wife.'

At the close of day, much communication had been exchanged, either by telephone home (a £15 card lasted ten minutes), or by talk in the two ships' bars, where the rate was far better. Now berthed alongside *Bransfield*, this even rarer spectacle was viewed from the water by the discerning few who had rigged and deployed their boat for the privilege.

Seeing people leave is always unsettling. For some the gangway was being used as an exit from *John Biscoe* and an arrival aboard *Bransfield*. The movement of personnel can be a minefield of complications, demanding diplomacy and tact. The crossflow of crew was an achievement in such considerations. Adjusting to their new circumstances, each would find the

At Port Stanley, *Bransfield*'s cargo for Rothera base is trans-shipped to *John Biscoe*. (Author's collection)

familiar act of packing and unpacking a foundation to ease the change. For those remaining, it was novel to see former colleagues working elsewhere, subtly members of a different team. They were glad not to be involved in the lengthened work programme, and *Bransfield* offered a northward passage to suit their needs; some were to stand by the new ship after their leave, and for John the second officer this meant a return to college to complete his master's qualifications. Having served for four full seasons as a crewman on *Bransfield* he was now returning as an experienced officer, gaining the status through disciplined study and scholarship backing, in recognition of effort. His face creased in a smile as he recalled his halcyon days as a hand on the Isle of Wight ferries. Little could he have known the future scope of his travels.

For the present, I was content to journey locally, in pursuit of a Golden Chance. The wrecked fishing boat of that name was within easy walking distance. Together with its neighbour, its slumped repose in the quiet shallows offered scope for a different kind of travelling, the movement of charcoal across paper, and with it an artistic reverie away from the present. Becoming immersed in the problems of perspective and tone offered the bliss of relaxation. The scratch of charcoal and the forming image were as a balm and key to a slower, simpler pace. It gave time to stare.

Freed for a few hours from the cares and claustrophobic intensity of ship life, grappling with different perspectives brought many others down to size. In a very different frame of mind from arrival, I was glad to be aboard when the ship left for sea. All ears were recovering from the noisy departure, hailed by tradition on the whistle. *Bransfield* added her own voice in send off, as we parted company and sailed beyond sight.

I am not very mechanically minded. It was with trepidation that I approached the subject of fuel filters. Donated from the now redundant stock of craft on *Bransfield*, an inflatable boat had been added to our collection. Space was getting cluttered. One boat had to be dismantled and the choice seemed easy. The one with the slow mysterious leak was reduced to its component parts and scattered to storage. It was a pity that we did not learn of a similar slow leak in the inherited boat.

Boats have a habit of consuming time, whether from choice or necessity. It was time to grapple with my fear; fuel filters were not going to spoil my day. Mustering tools, rubber tubes, hose-clips and visits to the engine room all brought slow progress. In the boat's stern a seeming tangle of wreckage gradually melded into a pleasing arrangement of pipes and brackets. In their places, the fuel filters sat like hearts behind the ribcage of their protecting plates. The lifeblood of fuel would flow healthily to the demands of the engine. In my small triumph I quelled the notion of becoming an engineer.

In the galley Shaun could pretend to be a master baker, as he was introduced to the pleasures of making bread. Across the divides of our roles aboard ship a broad education was exercised. Enlisted to work his passage home, cyclist Don had hung up his hat as messman to become a deckhand. He applied his quiet, unflappable humour to the new tasks, happier at the prospect of the invigoration of fresh air.

Across the funnel top the strengthening night-time wind blew like a bellows, liberating a streaming shower of sparks to cause a flicker of alarm. Ringing the engine room, no cause could be found, and they seemed unperturbed. I could cope with the elemental wind but would never make an engineer.

The lub' oil scavenge pump needed urgent attention. Reduced to one engine for the process, the weather could have been kinder for the repair. Clutching the gleaming brass wheel, the helmsman was as comfortable as any, and it was a rare event to be in control of the rudder's movement. In the storm he held the bows more readily into the seas than the autopilot, able to quickly apply full helm against the uncomfortable effects of falling off the wind.

Our destination on King George Island lay to the south. The westerly gale had fetched up seas of a size to preclude a bearable passage. As winds are wont, it swung southerly and began to build a new terrain of waves. In a growing lumpy confusion they jostled with the swell in which no comfort was found. Following the repair the decision to proceed was inevitable. At least it marked progress, no matter how laboured.

In the spray's periodic deluges the engine room was advised to fully close its skylights 'or you'll get more cooling water than you bargained for'. The barograph pen traced a near-vertical rise, yet it was among the steadiest of instruments, held fast in its chart room cradle. Elsewhere, cabins were being rearranged by the cavalier hand of violent erratic movement. Metal deadlights were lowered across portholes, sturdy plates to guard against shattering glass and the flooding intrusion of the elements. As the lookouts changed, glad to escape the airless interior, they joked at having been flung off a chair, and the sliding antics of the mattress that made a mockery of sleep.

Its handiwork complete, the wind all but died away, leaving our crazed lurching to seem the more bizarre. The catering officer lamented the damaged bond and the costly seepage of fine spirits to waste. For the first time in the trip, and with assurance of its effect, I took a substantial but legal dram. It was weather for power-assisted sleep.

Not all radar targets are icebergs, but in Antarctica's vast arena of wilderness the assumption is easily made. The isolated blip on the screen to the south-west depicted Bridgeman Island, clearly to be seen on the horizon. It alluded to the distant Bass Rock, which guards the approaches to the Firth of Forth. Its peppering of snow could, with a little imagination, be the clamorous colony of breeding gannets on lofty summer slopes. Lured by such easy comparisons, seeing a ship came as a surprise.

It appeared as if to chastise my assumptions, a gentle slapped wrist to pay closer attention to radar targets. On our opposite course, the Spanish tug *Neptunia* provided a distant focus of movement to tempt other surprised eyes to the bridge. A brief call on the radio established her identity. Having completed her own work at the adjacent islands, she was bound for Montevideo and warmer climes. Humbled as always by the accented English, I responded in native tongue, advising of our movements and stormy labours across the Drake Passage. In the days ahead, other vessels were to be seen at much closer quarters. The lesson had been timely.

A full two months having passed since our Christmas anchorage in the South Shetlands, the area had evidently seen more snow, as the ship's afternoon passage followed the south coast of King George Island, before making the expanse of Maxwell Bay. At its head, Fildes Bay remained hidden. Grouped around its crescent shores, bases of different nations clustered in neighbourly company: China, Uruguay, the Soviet Union and Chile. We were destined for the Chilean establishment of Teniente Marsh. Such concentration of civilisation needs maritime support. The Spanish ship *Las Palmas* added visual warmth from her orange hull and colourful flag. Anchoring nearby, salutations were exchanged. The newcomers grasped the extent of the settlements, exclaiming at the sight of a van moving between the buildings, and a snowcat lumbering its tracked way purposefully along a crushed highway of grimy snow.

'You should get shelter in the lee of the island' was a considerate thought aimed at the boat crews, but the elements had other ideas. The two inflatables hung off the base with slight dismay. The onshore wind tumbled sizeable waves against the little jetty. Standing in a huddle awaiting pick-up, the three-man party sensed it would not be an easy transfer to the ship, despite her proximity. The painful lash of biting spray on the face was endured in good humour, as mundane conversation was shouted in defiance of the lack of shelter. Beneath the canopy, snug as I thought in its protecting case, my camera was already swimming. For once I was to regret the photographer's maxim: if you don't take your camera you'll regret it. Later, back at the ship and with forlorn hope, the lens sat submerged in a sink of fresh water, its delicate innards beyond the reach of cleaning. Two of the newly collected personnel would soon be landed in the hidden interior of Deception Island for a month, to carry out a very different kind of cleaning – the assembling of historic detritus from the former whaling station.

With a slow plunging motion and a careful speed, *John Biscoe* began her dusk exit of Maxwell Bay. In the twilight, the backlit glimmer of the snow cliffs silhouetted *Las Palmas* as she passed by, her navigation lights piercing the gloom.

The Spanish support ship *Las Palmas* near the Fildes Bay multinational research complex on King George Island. (Author's collection)

'If to your starboard red appear it is your duty to keep clear.' The well-versed phrases of Thomas Gray are still as good an aid to memory now as when they were first written. Referring to two powered ships crossing, the rule-of-the-road regulations define it more soberly. Rule 15: 'When two power-driven vessels are crossing so as to involve risk of collision, the vessel which has the other on her own starboard side shall keep out of the way and shall, if the circumstances of the case admit, avoid crossing ahead of the other vessel.' In the first twelve weeks of bridge watchkeeping on *John Biscoe*, I had had no recourse to this otherwise commonly applied rule. It was an amazing irony to meet its demands in such a remote location. Intent on reaching Potters Cove, the Chilean support ship boldly displayed her red sidelight. The fate recognised in the writings of Rudyard Kipling succeeded in bringing us towards the same spot for the same time. In the confines of the bay, movement of the helm and easing of speed allowed the formless shape to pass ahead unhindered. For the rest of the night the radar targets were icebergs.

* * *

Nothing saps the energy better than an outboard motor unwilling to start. Returned to Negro Hill, off the Byers Peninsula, the cache of heavy equipment had been backloaded into the boats. In the early morning sun, the ship looked small and bright, beyond the feathered spindrift of the off-lying reefs. Waterborne once more, the weary muscles were steeled to one last effort. A hefty pull on the starter rope should bring the warmed engine to life. After half a dozen, the language waxed as the dregs of energy waned. It was then that I noticed the fuel pipe, severed by an unwitting blow, quietly emptying the tank contents onto the bottom-boards. The anchor heaved over the side to slow our drift on to rocks; the other boat towed us to safety. Reconnected, and with a quiet prayer, the healthy roar came as sweet music, and the prospect of a well-earned breakfast thankfully became imminent. The main scientific party, established at their temporary station two months previously, and since depleted in numbers following the visit of HMS *Endurance*, hoped that breakfast for them would be the last they consumed in their tents.

The lengthy passage around Snow Island was made in clear and benign conditions, affording a rare glimpse of the white glory of Smith Island. On the unclimbed 7,000-foot peak of Mount Foster, a Joint Services expedition was even yet trying to gain its summit. Returned by early afternoon to the anchorage in New Plymouth Sound, the tiny forms of the orange tents could be seen by a keen eye. At the shore, stockpiles of equipment had been built with much effort, standing patiently as penguins for the next move.

The smiles were genuine on both sides. In our own business and travels aboard ship, thoughts had returned to those left behind, and of what their lives had entailed in the interim. The greetings and humour evaporated the interval. Immersed jointly in the tasks of breaking camp, it was a social occasion to unite all hands. Cargo nets were spread wide across the boats. Food boxes, long emptied of victuals, now held samples of rocks, delicate plants and mud cores. Marshalling the loading, general assistant Paul confidently radioed requirements to the boat crews and the ship: these items are fragile, these are for the cool store, stow this general cargo for Signy. Reception in the hold found them duly dispersed and tallied.

All rubbish had been carefully bagged and the place left respectfully as it had been found. Cleaning up the wanton neglect of others, the jetsam from foreign fishing boats was also combed from the strandline. They were sickening symbols to disgust and stir disquiet for the future of this unique wilderness. Striking the tents and bearing their weighty bulk towards the shore called for extra assistance. Boatloads of willing helpers took the invigorating ride to be a part of the process. Such was our luck with the weather that there was no thought of stopping. The four boats plied for six hours, accompanied by low-flying terns, petrels and blue-eyed shags, bright in contrast with their drab northern relatives.

In the cool of evening the last two boats raced, full throttle held open in an iron grip as the waves were willed to submission. Salt-encrusted faces cracked into smiles, acknowledging the day's achievement, and left wondering how the day had begun. Negro Hill and the unwilling engine had surely belonged to yesterday!

It was the last day of February and all seemed well with the world, as our rejoined companions enjoyed afresh the novelty of cruising in southern waters aboard a well found ship. As the sound of engines rapidly faded signalling a significant easing of speed, the pleasurable sense of a secure freedom was jolted. In an instant, bridge-wings were filled with enquiring faces. I tried not to view them as a vote of no confidence.

Exploring unfrequented waters, it was only prudent to treat the echo soundings with respect. The up-rearing line levelled off at an ample depth. Shortly afterwards, and forewarned by the sonar, the next peak was more alarming. Full astern on the engines even brought the chief engineer up the stairs. A pinnacle at ten fathoms betrayed an interesting seabed. We had neither the time, nor a navigator's nerve left, to engage in a spot of surveying. Seeking deeper water further off the coast of Snow Island, we left the visible rocky stacks behind, and their extensive relatives lurking beneath the waves. Clearly it was a day for deceptions.

Visible in the distance, our destination seemed obvious enough. Yet it is not called Deception Island for nothing. It is well named, as is Sail Rock which we were to pass closely en route. Alone, and gently leaning, its strange and slender form sat dark on the horizon, looking truly as a yacht's canvas, hauled taut and sailing hard. Fully 7 miles from the coast of our destination it was a fitting outlier to prime our perceptions of Deception. We had read about this island of intrigue in the Admiralty Pilot Book.

Informed of its visual deceit did not lessen our anticipations. Volcanic in origin, Deception forms one of the largest and most remarkable crater islands in the world. Annular in shape and some 8 miles in diameter, it encircles a vast basin, an enclosed sea all but severed from the surrounding ocean save for a tiny gap in the rim. Named by American sealers as Neptune's Bellows this sole access to the interior is narrow and steep sided. Exposures of strata added colourful warmth of dark reds and ochres to the entrance cliffs, contrasting with the dull grey expanses of snow.

An area of shallows in mid-channel forced the ship to keep close beneath the northern vertical precipice. Brooded over by such a presence the unfolding prospect, when it came, was the more spectacular. The secret of Deception lay open before us; the huge bowl of Port Foster. A tiny alcove in its broad rim, Whaler's Bay nestles adjacent to the entrance. A sharp swing brought us within its confines. Signs of settlement and calamity bore witness to past events, while the clouds of steam rising from the water's edge gave a hint of an island sleeping uneasily.

Whaler's Bay, Deception Island. Here, on the former runway, Captain Elliott scattered the ashes of pioneering Antarctic aviator Group Captain J. H. Lewis. (Author's collection)

Tilted storage tanks and a collapsed hut were signs of the damage to this former British base, by the eruption of 1969. Standing intact, a huge hanger would no longer protect the aircraft which used to over-winter within its cavernous space. It lay adjacent to the site of the former runway which lined up with a narrow and plunging gap in the craggy skyline. Through this portal, known as Neptune's Window, aircraft flew in final approach and landing. In disbelief, at our anchorage we imagined the pilot's view and nerve, and the appearance from nowhere of an aeroplane navigating such a constriction. In our own approach to the bay we could at least afford to stop, and start again.

At 1800 GMT, standing alone on the runway and facing Neptune's Window, Captain Elliott scattered the ashes of Group Captain J. H. Lewis. The day was blustery and overcast with a continuous fall of light snow; probably not a time for flying. As navigators, each in their own professions, the Antarctic linked them in their chosen workplace. A greatly admired and larger-than-life character in both spirit and physique, Group Captain Lewis was the first pilot to fly over the South Pole in a single-engine aircraft and led the air support for two Antarctic expeditions. He was awarded the Polar Medal. Named after him, Mount Lewis and the Lewis Chain afford tributes to his memory.

Regardless of the chill and the snow fall, work continued. Two people were to be landed for a month, to clean up and package wastes for removal on our return. In addition to their needs for a comfortable stay, two All Terrain Vehicles and trailers aided their tasks. Transferred easily by the derricks from the hold into the awaiting barge, offloading them ashore needed more basic resource. Four bulky timbers provided a steep-ramped track-way for the machines to be driven up and over the stern. The finer points of the barge's construction revealed their purpose in providing a supporting anchorage for the ramps.

Weighing anchor in the early evening, from the decks spectators craned their necks at the towering heights and looked ahead through the defile of Neptune's Bellows to the grey neutrality of open sea beyond.

* * *

The term 'scenic route' was being bandied about with casual ease. In the Antarctic Peninsula, it means different things to different people. To the observers on board, and to those off duty, it brought a pictorial panoply of tortuous channels littered with ice, awesome peaks in unremitting parade and the occasional glimpse of base huts in impossible locations. In their unhindered freedom to observe, the viewers could also enjoy the porpoising

At Deception Island, the ship's workboat and scow-barge take vehicles and equipment to shore, for the environmental clean-up and eventual removal of old wastes. (Author's collection)

Deck trainee David Miles acts as a winchman during offloading. (Author's collection)

antics of penguins, the reluctance of seals to move off ice floes beneath our overshadowing bows, and the arching backs of whales. To the navigator it was also there, but snatched enjoyment was earnt. A 'scenic route' called upon the consistent skills that constrain the eyes of pure appreciation. Shutting off the exclamations of marvel that emanated from the bridge-wings and the faces that peered through windows onto the chart table, sense was constantly gleaned from the outward vista and the promises on the chart, as the ship was guided round many other obstructions.

It was to be a passage of superlatives, truly a day to remember as we headed south for Faraday base. The broad Gerlache Strait would have offered a direct route. Sinuous within its southern shores, our courses catered to the convolutions of winding passages – back alleys off the rare beaten track. By Danco Island, the curve of the Errera Channel led. Across Andvard Bay into Paradise Habour, the glory of ice sculptures lay suspended in its secretive enclosure. Through Ferguson Channel and by the outlying sentinels of Boutan Rocks, the southern limit of Gerlache Strait was joined. As with the right whales off South Georgia, we had been touched and humbled by the symbols and reality of this last and greatest wilderness. Supremely aloof and

Concentrated navigation in challenging waters: with bridge watches 'doubled', at the radar, chief officer Robin Plumley gives directional advice... (Author's collection)

...and obtains visual bearings with a gyro compass repeater. (Author's collection)

dominating, it is yet so fragile to the exploitations of humankind, and our unique ability to ruin. It was a fitting time and place to meet *Gondwana*, a potent envoy of our capacity to also care for our environment.

Rumour was rife that she was nearby. Discovered as a tiny entity, she was also highlighted in the sun; a glimpse of red hull separated her from the ice in which she moved. The Greenpeace ship was northbound, and by chance our paths were to coincide. Once more our decks were cluttered with viewers. There was a magnetism beyond simply sighting another vessel. We were registering an approval and an admiration. At such a moment none could wish other than that Antarctica should be a World Park. As a guardian, we hailed *Gondwana* and dared to think that *John Biscoe* had contributed to the same ideal.

It was a moment for a flourish of seamanship, as in the open water we swung sharp about to parallel her course. Familiar banter on the radio spoke of old acquaintances. In line abreast we kept close company before a noisy farewell. Soon she was lost to sight as we aimed our own course towards the pull of Capstan Rocks, oblivious to the special rendezvous the two ships were later to make in the cause of stewarding the continent's wildlife.

The extent of Capstan Rocks seemed greater than charted and we were drawn to make investigation. Donning the hats of hydrographers we indulged in a spot of surveying. Viewing the distant rocky humps from different points, putting them in transit and taking careful bearings, the charted information was variously verified and modified.

Checking the latest information supplied to the Admiralty, as producers of charts, we had to smile. *Gondwana* had been busy surveying, too, in addition to her primary role in monitoring man's destructive habits. We resumed our passage. Faraday base on the Argentine Islands awaited our attention.

The twin peaks are legendary, as much by name as by appearance. Guardians of the northern end of the incomparable Lemaire Channel, the astounding sight of the colloquially named 'Oona's Tits' marks Cape Renard. Lofty and well endowed, these tremendous mountain pillars proudly thrust skyward from sea level to well over 2,000 feet, then to be brushed by the silky touch of clouds. Several miles distant, and squeezed between the Graham coast and Booth Island, the alluring narrows of Lemaire Channel were approached with awe. The peaks on either hand were the closest ever to draw our eyes towards the zenith.

Soon after, eyes were peering downwards as the brakeman lowered each lifeboat towards the water. Their bottoms had not been wetted for some time, and they were ripe for immersion. It was an unbeatable location for a full boat drill and there were no moans at the prospect. The ship lay in a dazzling breathless calm. Three lifeboats sat alongside as the motley crews were marshalled to their cramped posts. The lengthy boathook was passed forwards, heavy oars were unlashed and raised vertically, crutches were shipped in the gunwales.

The extraordinary peaks at Cape Renard guard the approaches to the Lemaire Channel. (Author's collection)

Southbound, nearing Lemaire Channel narrows, with Faraday base beyond. (Author's collection)

Safely through the narrows. (Author's collection)

'Maurice is stroke oar, take your timing from him; starboard oars, do you know what "back-water" means?' Eager faces gazed expectantly astern. To the command 'bear away bowman!' the boathook was strained. After a false start, the starboard oars managed to back-water, and the port oars, next to the ship, lowered when they could. 'Give way together!' brought an ungainly flailing of oars by the uninitiated scientists until a rhythm was established. 'In, pull, out, feather,' the orders were jovially shouted. I was warming to the theme, as the controlling tiller influenced the boat's direction. 'Toss oars!' does not mean to throw them away, but to bring them smoothly to the vertical. A technique demanding practice, it was less than perfection that brought them thus. The boat engine sprang into enthusiastic life, and with a deafening roar shuddered the laden boat into reluctant movement. In the still water the boats were put through their paces. Like a proud mother duck, the ship lay attentive, her offspring eagerly meandering yet alert to the signs of recall. Recovery was laborious but duty had been done, and enjoyment had in the process.

The last miles led us with serenity through Penola Strait, bounded on the one hand by mountains and glaciers and on the other by a chain of low islands. Faraday nestled within the archipelago of these, the Argentine Islands. As with other bases, its location appeared beyond the close reach of the ship, yet soon *John Biscoe* would be precisely moored only yards off the rocks, at their very doorstep. It was well to approach the Meek Channel, the tight navigable way in to our destination, meekly. The entrance guarded

Mindful of the ship's extreme isolation, regular fire and abandon ship drills are given due importance. (Author's collection)

by the shoal of Corner Rock, it was paid due regard, bringing the ship hard by the ice-cliffs of Corner Island proper. With both anchors spread and ropes to the shore, *John Biscoe* lay across the channel. At that moment the narrows displayed a mild temperament, but were to reveal another side to their nature before we left.

For the present in benign mood, the sunset tinted the mountains to a roseate blush. In the fading dusk, the full moon rose, turning the chill twilight crystal silver. The window lights of Faraday augmented those of the ship to friendly warmth. Our communities had linked, as Colin and Don plied the launch for crossings of two-way visitors, before they too could relax at the day's end.

* * *

Oil drums are awkward brutes, regardless of their contents. Handled like oversized milk churns, the adept can balance one on a rim and hurl it into a tight stow, mindful of fingers being crushed. George, the bosun's mate, was an expert at it, and demonstrated his powers with confidence. Many were to learn much of the handling, stowage and securing of cargo under his humorous direction, and the lilt of a Scottish tongue. The oil drums became submissive in the grip of chains, lying dormant while being slung by derrick, yet missed no chance to thud against coaming, or spin to knock the unwary off footing. In clusters of four they were raised from the hold and lowered into the scow for delivery to shore. Awaiting their arrival, muscle-power and ingenuity were marshalled. There was no luxury of a hoist to make light of heavy loads.

Up the long planks and down, each drum was handled, a rope parbuckle used as a helpful purchase, an old technology of reliable effect. Animated figures bent low while propelling their cylindrical charges up-slope and in to store. Throughout the day, cargo was discharged and backloaded. Into the lower hold went wastes of all descriptions. It was added to as the voyage progressed, a refuse collector to augment the ship's list of functions.

The box was labelled 'Books for Biscoe'. It arrived unannounced. On opening later, a treasure chest of many old hardback books called for shelf space. For some, they would offer fresh reading, though with paperback collections and a library supplied by the Marine Society, many tastes were already catered for.

A foretaste of things to come, the bergy bit crept stealthily nearer. As an icy form, it was all sensuous curves, weathered by time and the relentless smoothing of waves. In Meek Channel it had found a quiet backwater and was content to drift at the whim of wind and current, or ground on the rocky bed. Its wanderings were viewed with suspicion. Would it nudge the ship broadside, or pass safely ahead? With a slow majesty it deigned to ignore the ship, merely clipping an anchor cable in passing. By evening it had enlisted a conspirator. On the return journey, they were sizing up to cause trouble.

Lying peacefully alongside, the launch was prone to attack. It was time she was elsewhere. Mustered to her rescue the crew backed her clear of the danger. Minutes later the blunt-nosed battering ram struck with a ponderous weight that would have crushed the launch. Absorbing the shock, the ship gently recoiled, and the crumpled scar of impact appeared as a blooded nose to the snout of the assailant. Content to lean against the ship, moves needed to be made. As David to Goliath, the launch made a daring approach. Impudent in her eagerness, after minutes of fruitless pushing she began to impart a reluctant momentum. By slow inches the ice was coaxed to pivot round the bow, its underwater bulk keen to grasp at the straining anchor cables. Sent on its way, once more in the gentle tidal stream, the launch turned to face the remaining foe. In the fading light, the sound of her valiant engine was all that could be heard. Fascinated, spectators watched as the little drama was enacted. The third engineer and second officer discussed their own encounters in other waters. Water cannon can deflect approaching ice. In protecting valuable oil rigs, bergs can be lassoed and towed clear by the long-suffering vessels that guard their environs. Well pleased with her night's work, the launch jauntily resumed her timetable in carrying passengers, barely minutes late in her schedule. She would be travelled in with renewed affection, a little ship of fresh renown. Many years into the future, as Harbourmaster's launch *Biscoe Kid*, she would be present as part of the official flotilla on the River Thames celebrating the Queen's Diamond Jubilee.

As on arrival, Meek Channel was kind to us. No awkward breezes blew to complicate our departure. Recovering each anchor cable in turn was marked by a plodding progress as the heavy 'gypsy' gripped and hauled each link before sending it below into the cavern-like hold of the chain locker. In lying prone across the narrow channel, the unwelcome hand of the breeze could swing the ship towards shore. At the stern, with time to stare as the ropes were coiled down, the illusive hues of green could be appreciated around the exposed rocky islets. Thick mosses grew in profusion, and the polished edges of overlying ice were stained by the bloom of algae. On this archipelago the ice was retreating. To periodic visitors, its disappearance brought a fresh aspect to stimulate memory. Time was when the whole of Grotto Island was under a blanket of ice. Hanging in the wardroom, the old photograph verified these words, and showed *John Biscoe* also changed from her present form, evolution to mark the passage of time. The photograph had been taken thirty-two years previously, almost to the day. It depicted Meek Channel and Penola Strait congested with ice. Faraday was a simple collection of huts. A new ship, only on her third voyage south, *John Biscoe* hid her newness behind a shield of her silhouette. Shown in company with two US icebreakers, the little convoy was soon to toil and suffer. Released from being held fast in ice and towed by *Northwind*, the excesses of her assistance tore out the securing point at the bows. Pencilled in the rough log, the account was brief, belying the drama: 'Forward starboard fo'c'sle bitts carried away'.

Back in the present, northbound in the Penola Strait, it was a source of wonder to see the spindly forms of two masts. Tucked in at a tiny bay on Petermann Island, the vulnerable grace of the yacht spoke of cares beyond our own, of an even closer affinity to the joys and troubles of this demanding environment. As if in demonstration, the Lemaire Channel bore a tattered carpet of ice not present on our previous passage. Like a finger drawn across a misty pane, the ship's gentle progress left a dark and restrained track. Noisily the brash of ice rasped the sides and tinkled in a tuneless brittle carillon. On small floes, leopard seals ignored our presence or surged with a sleek rippling of flesh, seeking safety in the oily stillness of sea.

The emblematic peaks of Cape Renard retreating astern, ahead lay the bulk of Anvers Island. On its southern coast, Biscoe Point and Biscoe Bay were to pass within sight, as the highway to Neumayer Channel was sought. Lying between Anvers and Wiencke Island, on this occasion it was to be a user-friendly waterway, deep and clear of obstruction, but mysterious in all its winding aspect. On a jutting isthmus, the British base of Damoy peeped from beneath the weight of the black mountains at its rear. Mute spectators held their thoughts as they glimpsed the tiny-looking buildings and reckoned them against the enormity of their surroundings. The same eyes looked quizzically ahead, the ship seemingly intent on a full-speed passage into a landlocked, rocky and mountainous oblivion. Reluctantly, it gave up its secret, as a channel snaked a narrowing course towards its confluence with the broader Gelache Strait. Its own litter of islands and angular indented coasts led past the solitary flashing light on Bell Island, prompting queries as to who maintains such an isolated but welcome beacon. Through our own dark hours, and in future days, the light would blink, as a rare alpine flower may bloom in a mountain crevice, unseen by appreciative eyes.

Throughout the following day, the touch of the first fingers of approaching winter spun an icy cocoon about the weather-side rails and rigging. Beyond the shelter of the Bransfield Strait, the wind-flung spray swept through the freezing air and clung by slow layers about the exposed wires and latticework of guardrails. From these hung an icicled drape, seen as a canvas dodger to the swift glance. The accumulations obliterated detail and swelled familiar forms into grotesque caricature. The decks and hatch were petrified beneath a heavy glaze which turned real canvas to iron and taut rope to bars of steel.

It was an exciting transformation. An unusual occurrence, it melded the right combination of conditions: a cold wind of a strength to send spray aboard, and a temperature below the freezing point of seawater. This is one cause that can lead to icing on ships' hulls and superstructures. If severe enough, it can be a serious danger, adversely affecting a ship's stability. Extreme cases have resulted in capsize. Our own encounter was mild by comparison, but it was to keep the crew busy in making escape from its grip. A variety of tools was wielded, attacking with relish a cluster that would shatter into a spectacular shower of shards, or chiselling with care into angular recesses. It brought a dim reminder of shovelling the drive clear at a distant home.

It was on 5 March that the captain intimated to Darren, the astounded lookout, 'I was twenty-two once.' In conveying his birthday congratulations,

Ice accretion is promptly removed to maintain the ship's stability. (Author's collection)

the moment of reflection was shared on the bridge-wing, dispelling the veneers of seniority and forging a common link. It was substantial, the recollection being that he, too, had passed that particular milestone on the *John Biscoe*. With relaxed ease, they warmed to the common theme. In the chill of the invigorating breeze, Darren responded with tales from his recent time on *Bransfield*. Had he remained, instead of transferring, he would be feeling a balmy breeze to herald warmer days, as that ship approached Montevideo on her long voyage back to the UK.

Our eyes were wary of ice but, unlike the previous passage to Signy, none was to be seen, save on the very threshold of the islands. Hidden in its secretive den of Factory Cove, Signy once more aroused curiosity. The doctor, whose home it was to become, scrutinised the blank headland with its solitary beacon light, intense even in the brightness of day. Sunshine Glacier glowed with inner radiance, the Borge Bay bergs were stately in their static parade, and the immediate hinterland of Signy a delicate relief thanks to a mottled peppering of new-fallen snow.

Seeing the ship caused raised eyebrows and the levelling of binoculars. A large commercial vessel, lying at anchor further out in the bay, her task was as mother to the fishing craft that had kept our second officer occupied in the early hours. As if disturbed by our intrusion, she soon slipped away.

The wind was to be master of our fates, dealing us precise and bitter blows to frustrate all efforts at mooring safely off the base. As time was pressing, the opportunity offered by a mid-morning lull was seized. The rope-handling teams from shore were borne to their exposed outcrops as the ship's anchor was shortened in its stay. Oaths greeted the gusts, and the decision wavered. A Force 9 would brook no argument; the complex mooring in the tight confines of the cove was not to be attempted. Everybody stood down to play the waiting game once more.

There was another chance several hours later, but the moment faded as, with disbelief, the onrush of sweeping snow fell to obscure the wider world, driven by the fury of a different gale. Unsafe in the previous anchorage, the tedium of repositioning brought a dragged anchor. As it plunged to the seabed, the depth was noted and the ship's position obtained. Sailing in the wind, it was disconcerting to imagine the weighty anchor scrabbling with fluked fingers to grasp and stay our motion. Success came slowly; we tested our luck no more. The locked cases of mail were dispatched ashore by launch to bring succour to the scientists at close of day.

* * *

Looks were incredulous. How dare there be a fault! How could there be? We span the wheel for the third time in twenty-four hours; the ritual was usually a trouble-free precursor of impending action. To sense its erratic grip, soft to the hand instead of firm, cried out that there was a problem. It did not auger well for third time lucky in mooring off the base. Too soon in the day, yet more oaths were being muttered against ill luck. Clustered around the wheel, with its bulky brass chamber of oil and pipework, an enquiring bedside manner was adopted to determine the ills of the mute patient. The oil reservoir was dipped, the wheel flexed and, in the remoteness of the stern, the humming steering motors and linkages were scrutinised. By slow degrees, the wheel's spongy lethargy was dispelled as, by the therapy of several hands, the circulation of oil was returned to a warm and full-blooded flow, urging the rudder to turn on command.

With minds primed by this minor drama, the major business of the day resumed. This was the final visit of the season to Signy, and for *John Biscoe* her very last. Invitations for meals flowed freely from ship and shore. The galley forgotten, the cooks laboured to prepare lunches that would remain uneaten. 'Eleven have gone ashore' was greeted by the second cook's irony – 'That's nice for them' – as he surveyed the unwitting excess of food.

At evening, in the wardroom the base commander and other shore guests provided a stimulation of yarn and humour. They were pleased at a new audience and did not stint in the telling of misadventure and ribbing of colleagues. Into their midst, from the long-suffering cooks a symbol of their confectioner's art was delivered. It was a tribute to their boss, Hamish, on his fortieth birthday. The cake, with its many cherries, was soon demolished. It was to be the first of several such celebrations in the month of March.

The thankless and un-relished task of prising all appropriate people back to the ship fell to the second officer. In their cosy reverie, levering them into the chill of night and on to the bucking launch was a matter of relentless extrication. For some, the moment was poignant. Home to scientists for two years, the farewells to departing members was genuine. The strobe flash of cameras pierced the smoky pallor of hand flares and rockets. Through this battle-like haze of red, the launch escaped, as if re-enacting a latter-day Dunkirk, but more certain of her safe return. The troops were well fed, and replete with pleasant memories.

Aboard ship the partings were equally protracted. In the wardroom, handshakes and thanks were repeated. Below the vacant windows, the crew lingered in the well deck cold. They chafed to lift the launch aboard, and set themselves at last to their own warm merriment beyond the beckoning portholes just feet away.

* * *

'I got blinding sun, rolling fog and growlers, all at once!' It was a doubtful welcome to the approaches to Washington Strait, our gateway through the eastern islands of the South Orkneys. 'You didn't expect to get them one at a time, did you?' the captain responded jovially to my bitter observation.

With Signy beyond sight astern, and a scenic passage off the coasts of Coronation Island, the morning was passing well. Ahead lay the challenge of Washington Strait to assure a watch of careful interest in the offing. Lying between Powell and Laurie islands it afforded means to strike northwards sooner, for our return to yet more dramatic locations in South Georgia.

To say Ailsa Craig to many seafarers brings memories of the Clyde, and the 'Paddy's Milestone' island that welcomes all to that Scottish haven. Our second officer responded by saying 'tomatoes'. The similarity was not obvious until his horticultural bent, and knowledge of plant varieties, explained the utterance. Whatever our tastes, an Ailsa Craig island lay not far distant, in company with many Scottish names that adorned the barbed shape of Laurie Island: Scotia Bay, Fraser Point and Mackenzie Peninsula. This last forms the eastern flank to the strait.

Shaping towards its coasts, hidden by enveloping cloud, the two grounded icebergs gave immediate visual impact. The erratic sun cast them into a glistening hue, impossibly bright, impossibly hard. Downwind of their enormous presence, and in the rising lop, I anticipated meeting growlers. The sun was otherwise unhelpful. What it revealed with one hand it obscured with the other. Our new course lay straight into its reflected path. With a well-timed conspiracy, a fog descended and the ship was slowed none too soon. The growler was cheated of its fun, but it had been a close thing. I was left to imagine the sickening impact, which would not have met with approval. The strait was followed with a weaving course. The clouds lifted to reveal glimpses of dull cliffs, then sank to obscure all. The radar image of Powell Island painted an indented coast rather different to the featureless sweep depicted on the chart. The discrepancy remained a mystery but brought a navigator's disquiet to the surface.

Seen simultaneously by lookout and watchkeeper, the sighting brought two responses. Accurately came the lookout's cry of 'whales', as I stifled my first thought: rocks! It was an inner fight with reason against the spectres that can jar nerves so easily into always thinking the worst. The positions marked on the chart and the pencilled times adjacent spoke of a brief ninety-minute passage through the strait. In its passing, time had also played its tricks.

***

The pastoral hues tried their best to appear welcoming but were overpowered by greater forces. At the western extremity of South Georgia, Bird Island lay small but with a proud boast of productivity in its wildlife. A central haven within its southern shores, Jordan Cove led to an inner sanctum of shelter, where the tiny scientific base is located. Affected by strong westerlies on our journey from Signy, problems were anticipated at Bird Island. Any winds from south or west would make the approach and anchorage untenable, on the brink of an exposed and hazardous coast. It was too much to hope for northerlies and the perfect shelter then afforded by the island. In grim fury, the wind blew to a peak of awkwardness. Of necessity hugging the coast, which loomed large and intimate, the patch of off-lying danger was passed, in its seething and heavily breaking turmoil. With a momentum fuelled by the adjacent slopes, the wind heeled the ship at her hard-won anchorage. Conditions worsened, allowing the easy and only decision: to postpone our visit. There was nothing lost in the attempt save the anticipation of a scientist ashore who needed medical and dental treatment. He viewed our departure with private pain. It took only minutes to vacate the confines and pass through Stewart Strait northwards. The captain smiled almost with apology as we gazed at the namesake danger which dictated our avoiding course. Elliott Rock was mirthless, as the blunt tooth gnawed the sea into white tatters.

Barely a half-mile off the northern shores, only the island's rock-girt feet protruded from beneath the curtains of cloud, as, with the wind now comfortably astern, we followed the coastal trend. Our new goal stirred special anticipation: Grytviken, so rich in history, event and lingering memorabilia. The six-hour passage off the coast of South Georgia was made with a fine speed and with a refined grandeur of the coastal prospect. Sights were revitalised in passing; glaciers, bays, headlands and mountains were as familiar friends, seen weeks previously during the programme of oceanography. It was with a particular pleasure that we sensed the acquisition of 'local knowledge', as names and their proper order sprang in answer to their sightings: Bay of Isles, Cape Saunders, Black Rocks.

No less exciting was the entrance to Cumberland Bay and with it the imminence of our destination, King Edward Cove. At its head lies the disused whaling station of Grytviken, compact in its decay, more constrained in its original design. Sentinel by the entrance at King Edward Point, the small British Army garrison appeared less than military. The white wooden buildings with red corrugated roofs spoke of a quaint camouflage. Towards its low jetty, barely feet above the tide level, the ship manoeuvred in a tight arc. Deployed with a precision very much military, the grim-clad soldiers took up strategic positions to act as our linesmen.

On the quay sat the object of our visit, a decompression chamber for divers, due to be shipped home for testing. Its cylindrical bulk craned aboard on to the after deck, the ship was moved astern for a more secure overnight mooring at the jetty. The operation highlighted a structural weakness in the concrete foundations, as the winch-hauled mooring ropes toppled a bollard. It was set to remain a doubtful souvenir of our visit and a task of repair to occupy the garrison's engineers.

Work completed and the engines silenced for the day, the ship's engineers emerged from the den of their own cares to observe their new surroundings with keen expressions. In the dank and descending gloom, some joined the walkers intent on exploring Grytviken. Beyond the rusting edifices, remote and preserved, the small wooden church stood in mute appeal, untainted in its bright paintwork, serene in its simple interior. The delicate spire acted as a kindly beacon to approaching vessels. Laid to a semi-submerged rest, two whale-catchers leaned in watery companionship at their supporting jetty. Their ruin was disguised by the tall woodbine funnels, recently painted in bright, banded colours. As an echo to this visual surprise the eye was drawn to a similar column of colour at the opposite end of the waterfront. Here, in statelier pose, the catcher *Petrel* floated on an even keel, her hull also rendered spruce by the application of a proper finish. As a museum piece, the background made her presence all the more striking.

The little graveyard did not shout out to be noticed, but in its isolation it was sought by those who wished the pilgrimage. Here, a particular grave exuded a touch of the noble. It was answered across the cove by a memorial cross, on the elevation of Hope Point. Beneath its simple form the words left out much: *Ernest Shackleton. Died January 5th 1922. Erected by his comrades.* It overlooks Cumberland Bay, stout to the feel of sea winds and to the peace that comes after storms. Among the greatest and most respected of polar explorers, it was a humbling moment to stand at his memorial. Jostled by the present wind, recollections of his feats demanded and received willing admiration. To have personally spent an accumulated year on a research ship named after him, brushed in her own time by the shades of earlier endeavours in the Antarctic, forged a link of latter-day appreciation.

Beyond Hope Point the sun shafts of the following day's dawn pierced the clouds. Behind Grytviken the high crags and slopes of scree were textured by a dusting of fresh snowfall. Oblivious to our early departure, the sleeping scientists were rudely awakened. This was not a place to leave anybody behind. 'Will you do a check on numbers?' was an easy request

At Hope Point, Grytviken;
the memorial to Sir Ernest
Shackleton. (Author's
collection)

to make. Disturbing slumber was less so. In the shared cabins, mixed
responses came from behind the bunks' obscuring curtains. None seemed
enthusiastic at the roll call, yet a few stalwarts emerged from their comfort
to witness our departure. The mechanics of letting go were subdued, in
deference to the stillness of morning. Taut ropes, suddenly released of their
tension, smacked their length noisily into the water, like a beaver's tail or
the fluke of a warning whale.

Less than two hours on a coastal passage found *John Biscoe* heading into
the familiar waters of Stromness Bay. The trio of former whaling stations
sat impartial to our intent. On this occasion our destination was Husvik,
the southernmost of the three. Boasting the luxury of a lengthy jetty, it was
nonetheless well guarded. Broadcast across the off-lying waters, shoals
and rocky outcrops, with their attendant mats of kelp, seemed to bar
any approach. On Bar Rocks the cardinal beacon proclaimed that Main
Channel lay to the south. Its lesser neighbours, Alert and Whaler channels,
defied the credibility of usage.

The jetty had seen better days. It gave the impression that it would
disintegrate should a vessel touch with more than a caressing nudge. Due

consideration applied, *John Biscoe* ghosted alongside. Members of the residing scientific party bade us greeting as we observed the products of their handiwork. A narrow and certain highway of boards ran the length of the rotting structure. They were bounded by the tracks of a narrow gauge railway upon which small wagons were to be pushed by hand, to bring the consignments of cargo to the ship's side. In returning the gangway to the stern by the dubious causeway, Lea was anxious for my safety. As we dragged its alloy bulk awkwardly across projecting snags he gallantly warned me of an impending plunge through rotten boards. No sooner said than his own foot found a weakness. Caught at the armpits he gave an unappreciative scowl to the general response, 'Come on, Lea, stop messing about!'

As wooden crates descended through the hatchway, upraised eyes in the hold watched their descent, a background of intense blue sky hinting that a glorious day was being missed in toil. At least our air was fresh, unlike for those ashore. As the empty wagons rattled their way back for further loads they disappeared into the dark interior of a large storage building. At the doorway the senses were assaulted by an acid stench. As eyes adjusted to the airless gloom the monstrous heaps materialised; the shed was a warm and dry wallow for mature male elephant seals. Vociferous and massively threatening in complaint, their aura ensured that nose-wrinkling encounters were kept brief.

A delicate mooring at Husvik. (Author's collection)

The seasonal scientific base at Husvik was being closed down and left deserted over the winter. At sailing time in the early afternoon only one person remained ashore, to let go the ship's lines. Adept and nimble, the bosun's mate fitted the bill. With sure footwork on the precarious jetty, the rope ends were eased from their bollards, carried weightily and free of tangles. As the stern swung clear, one pivotal rope remained, taut and vital. Casting this off with a flourish, no time was lost in getting aboard; swift departures were known to be enjoyed.

Sue was also enjoying herself. A departure from normal activity, cutting hair was a source for amusement and a means of refreshing some less demanding skills. In the Wet Laboratory aft the stage was set beneath bright lights and the gallery of windows with their parade of moving seascapes. A chair, assembled combs and scissors completed the improvised barber's shop. As straight and curly locks fell in their turn to the tiled deck, the recipients observed that they were sitting in a notable thoroughfare. There was little chance of a quiet trim, and ribaldry was rife. Satisfied customers acknowledged Sue's handiwork. 'Wash it, to get its full glory...'

The ship's progress led us into Elsehul. In company with the bosun's mate, and huddled from the breeze of the ship's forward motion, we sheltered in the lee of the foredeck, shadowy figures in the blackness of night, waiting the call to action. High overhead the searchlight beam probed forward, an intense comet tail across the backdrop of stars. In a looming silhouette of a deeper darkness, the ship's superstructure reared skyward, pierced by the warm subdued light of curtained windows. In the inscrutable wheelhouse beyond, navigational preparations were being made for our imminent arrival at the anchorage. Disembodied, the voice issued close to my ear. 'Stand by for'd!' broke the stillness as it crackled from the radio handset clipped to my lapel. Unseen from our hideaway, we clambered up the ladder to the foredeck. Heavily the anchor clanked as it was lowered and held above the water. Below, the bow wave sliced cleanly as the ship slowed. Ahead, the height of land brooded large, dimly lit from the searchlight's beam, cast upward from the sea's mirror surface. With an eerie textured form, the glow picked details of rock and chasm.

Beneath our feet the deck vibrated as the engines were put astern. Poised at the hefty brake handle, the order to 'let go' was not long in coming. The dust and echoes subsided as two figures leaned sharply over the rails with down-pointing torches to illumine the anchor chain-cable, patiently waiting for it to assume first an angled tautness, then the gently slackening curve to show that the anchor had held fast. Urged then to 'stand down', we could return to the homely world at the other side of the door.

* * *

The following morning inattentive observers may have missed our change of anchorage. *John Biscoe* still lay tethered, but it was in a different location from the previous night. At first light and but a short journey, the prospect of Bird Island once more greeted enquiring viewers. 'Bird Island base may only be small but it's a good one to have behind us.' The chief officer spoke with feelings awakened from previous years. In the course of the day we were to sample his meaning. Once again the weather was marginal for work to proceed. We waited in 'coiled spring' mode. Between ship and shore the sea seethed with cavorting seals. Don the watchman dryly noted, 'It should be called Fur Seal Island really.' Inquisitive, slippery-smooth and lithe in their activity, they opposed the fluffy stillness and aloof resignation of the albatross chicks on their island nests.

Activity was finally given the go-ahead. Now practised in their deployment, the launch and barge were swung from their cradles, the ship heeling and rocking gently upright in answer to the pendulous weight. A pair of inflatable boats kept close company, as a real and necessary security against the attentions of the seals. The convoy lurched its way into the fret of the little cove. Hidden behind the outreach of obscuring rocks, the drama unfolded. In the difficult holding ground, the barge's anchor did not take and was beyond safe control. Once again the conditions proved unworkable. The ship at her own anchorage also needed to be ready to escape. Barge, launch and boats were recovered. Agreement was universal: it would indeed be good to get Bird Island behind us.

On the second attempt there was no retreat. With the pace of activity, the calming of conditions passed almost without notice. Oily smooth and misty, the elements merged to envelop the toiling of many hands. The relief of the shore base was being made at the bottom of the glass, as the barograph ceased its fall. Completion stole upon us. Six hectic hours, and the base was left alone to continue its scientific contemplations of the wildlife that crowds upon its doorstep. To those aboard, having glimpsed its profusion, there was talk of the seals and the nesting albatrosses. They had left their indelible impression; Bird Island would not be forgotten.

It was 13 March 1991. I was old before my time, cheated in my prime by three hours. In a time zone where we lagged behind GMT, there lingered the embers of being aged thirty-four. I had forgotten the approach of the painful milestone but, as the GMT clock worked its way towards midnight, to spill into the chasm of another year, I found the message 'Happy Birthday, Trevor, from the Bridge Boys', slipped into the logbook.

No words had been spoken, but birthdays were spotted by the eagle-eyed. Nobody would slip through the net unnoticed. Some birthdays were planned for and heralded; others would take by surprise. On my desk, at our own midnight, the card waited patiently. As was the case for so many others before me, I had been discreetly observed by Alan, the electrical engineer. Trait and caricature were stored in his mind. The cards were fashioned with a delicate care by his own hands. At his desk, the pen and watercolour brush brought to life an image both amusing and wickedly accurate, though some might protest the extent of jowl, the protrusion of chin.

'You're beginning to look your age,' remarked Maurice as I pulled up a chair for breakfast. To rub in the salt of humour still further I was apprised of a poem. From the copious volumes of Robert Service, 'At Thirty Five' laughed up from the pages:

> Three score and ten, the Psalmist saith,
> And half course is well nigh run;
> I've had my flout at dusty death,
> I've had my whack of feast and fun.
> I've mocked at those who prate and preach,
> I've laughed with any man alive;
> But now with sobered heart I reach
> The Great Divide of Thirty Five.

The conspiracy to enforce maturity seemed relentless. Freed by the captain's courtesy to relieve the chief officer on watch for dinner, I dined at the main sitting, constrained in full uniform that added an unaccustomed weight. My natural age seemed sixteen; I mused that I was an intruder at too high a table. The cake, when it came, was a youthful reminder, a vast token from the galley staff, to be divided with relish about the ship. Demolishing cakes defies the decorum of age.

* * *

School adventures were generally marred by having to write up reports. The task always hung as a spectre to deny the perfection of escape. At the end of the day, homework required the recording of events. To some, such writing became a pleasure, an extension of experience. To others it was drudgery. For Brian, Sue and Paul it was a task to be shared. Returned from their two months as assistants to the scientific field party, with customary good planning they devolved the job at hand, each to their own strengths and interests. Thus, the aspects of travel, equipment and communications were hammered out in turn, to the insistent screen above the word processor. With sighs of gratification, their handiwork lay bound before them, product of a busy day.

Wearied from very different daytime tasks, David the watchman rose from his evening slumber at half past seven. He looked forward to breakfast before going on lookout duty. Confused in the mess-room, the body clock adrift by twelve hours, the tricks of time easily play havoc with those on combined shifts and day work. It was to be one of those nights. In the bridge darkness, finding a steadying nook between the consoles, a lurch from the sea pressed his weight forward, to find its fateful mark on the whistle push. The resultant strident jarring blast caused both our hearts to pound, and a query from below decks.

Captain Elliott happily ate his words at dinner. 'We've not seen any of the ladies in a dress.' The observation was soon laid to rest by Sue. Kept for special events and as a change to counter the workaday leggings, boiler suits or casuals, it was a two-way pleasure for the welcome guest to be so attired. As a breath of fresh air it spoke of images remote from life at sea.

Intense to the eyes, it was very much a sunset at sea. Our westerly course bore us straight down its avenue of dazzling reflection. Cruel as angled shafts spotlighting dust on polished furniture, the saltwater stains glistened on the bridge windows. Seeing ahead was far from easy. Hopes were high that the sun's slow plunge would reward the gazers with a green flash, the last colour to burgeon briefly at the horizon as the orb slipped from view. It was a novelty for first-timers, yet a disappointment that the flash was in reality just a momentary glow.

In the growing darkness, the eyes relaxed into a far-sighted and dilated demeanour, readily absorbing the formless expanse of sea above the partly whitened structure of the ship's bows. A curtain not drawn cast its cabin light with a waxing luminance on to the foredeck, once more to confound lookout and watchkeeper of their best night vision. Leaning over the dodger, the culprit cabin was identified, and the curtain drawn. With anticipation, the first lights of the Falklands were awaited. A tight cluster rose ahead and lingered at the horizon: the higher lights of Stanley. Cape Pembroke Lighthouse winked its regular message. Our landfall was made.

The discrepancy was noticed idly the following morning as the anchor was weighed in Blanco Bay. In the stillness of dawn, the low hills at this western extremity of Port William were featureless of the works of man, all except the beacon. A helpful day-mark, its light also ensured use in the dark hours. At the transition into day, the stab of green brightness caught the roaming eye and with it brought a frown. A glimpse at the chart confirmed

suspicion. The light was indicated as white, not green, a small point of
detail but the lot of a navigator's criticism. On another hillside, two posts,
each topped by a large coloured triangle, stood mysteriously apart on the
gently sloping ground, one lower than the other. Brought into line they
became united in purpose, as guide marks to lead users of the narrows
through into safety.

There was no evidence of breeze, often the helping hand that prevails
from the west. 'I can't get the stern in for love nor money!' remarked the
captain lightly, as, in a suspension of movement, the ship hung close to the
quay, her bow tethered to shore and steadied by an anchor. A breeze would
have gently urged the stern alongside. Instead it lay angled, taunting. The
tedious process of sending a rope ashore unaided across the gap finally
brought success. By dint of hauling power on the winch, the stern was
brought to heel, to lie obediently at the quayside. The logbook was sparse
of entries for the day: 'Taking fresh water periodically', 'Crew at leisure'
summed up the events. It was a time for a brief rest, for peace and quiet
earned.

* * *

'Turn that noise off NOW!' percolated uneasily through my sleep, rousing
me to gaze at my watch. It was one o'clock in the morning. As the alleyway
echo subsided, taking with it the wrathful pounding steps of a rudely
awoken chief officer, the thought came that rarely is a ship allowed to be
peaceful. The ruination of slumber came from shore visitors, intent on
mischief with their blaring ghetto blaster. Hotly pursued, the pair was seen
off the ship, and did not return.

It was a bad start to a musical day, but the intrusion slipped from
memory, with the anticipation of evening. In the town hall the Marine Band
would be playing. Enthusiastically, the chief engineer strode the coastal
path, to hear melodies different from the beat of well-running engines. A
harmony prevailed on the ship as through the afternoon the preparations
for St Patrick's Day were orchestrated. The Irish contingent – Ailbhe, Mike
and Maurice – rose to the occasion. The scientists' lounge was decorated
in orange and green. Little shamrocks were cut from coloured card and
issued with the personal touch. They doubled as invitation and entrance
ticket. Shamrocks must be worn, and wear something green, the notice had
said.

The second steward was girt about with a green duvet cover, in fine Roman
style for fancy dress. Mike appeared suitably as a leprechaun. Above our
heads and on vertical surfaces were stuck names of the Irish famous, and

obscure. The cans of stout were passed around freely as the strains of Irish folk and dance music kept feet and fingers tapping, and snatched lines were sung in recognition. The scramble of voices and melodies soon instilled its atmosphere. It was an easy fancy to think that we were truly under a roof on Erin's Isle. The chief engineer's penny whistle struck up melodiously, his eyes screwed shut in concentration below the green safety helmet. The feet of Ailbhe were rarely still, bright buckled in shamrocked shoes. She led the revellers in the dance. Hector and his accordion brought appreciative smiles. Head inclined and fingers nimble, jigs and reels cascaded from the keys. The dancing would have won no prizes, except for enthusiasm. In a tangled climax and the pause for breath came the ready wit: 'I thought that went rather well!'

Shanties and nonsense songs interspersed the jaunty festivity that made short work of time. All would agree next day that it had indeed gone rather well. Across all superficial divides, a new unity had been sown by the quiet and sharing patriotism of our friends. For the busy few days to come it was a fine start and a fitting farewell for the latest contingent to be returning home.

A certain lack of enthusiasm greeted the next morning, as the hatchways were opened into the lower hold. It was not an exotic cargo that needed offloading, but a tight-packed migraine of motley wastes that was a headache to all who donned hard hats and gloves, which quickly became ruined. Adopting the boyish bravado that raises laughter out of nauseous grime, pioneering inroads began to make an impact. On the quay, dumper trucks and flatbed wagons bore away the discharges to landfill, incineration or treatment.

In cabins, far from the communal rush, packing of a more pleasant sort occupied the lucky few. The time had come for them to go home. For others there was a transition, a halfway house in their forthcoming travels. Residing off-pay in the Falklands until the ship next returned for her own homeward passage, the four willingly accepted the new challenge. At a local farm, bed and board had been offered in exchange for work. It was to be a fascinating few weeks of experiencing a true flavour of real Falkland life.

A long journey often begins with waiting, a tedious lingering that suppresses movement and weighs heavily on the anticipation of travellers. On the after deck close to the gangway, the multicoloured luggage did little to cheer the blustery greyness of morning. 'The bus is coming at seven o'clock,' had caused an early stir in the scientists' quarters as they finally quit the small shared cabins. Parcelled into bulging rucksacks and bags, their belongings also seemed poised for a glimpse of Bob's white van. It was to be a loose schedule, and small talk was made with eyes frequently cast up the road.

A reflex response when the vehicle appeared, the languid attitudes were transformed into activity. Viv had set a daring precedent to be followed. A peck on the cheek to one meant similar treatment to all who had mustered for the send-off. As Bob finally mastered the lashing of the excess luggage and skis on the top of his vehicle, other crucial threads had already been severed. The travellers were intent on a very different road; their inner thoughts were no longer weaved with those who waved back their goodbyes.

In the evening, at the Malvina Hotel, thoughts of their airborne progress towards home did cause reflection. Indulging for once in a meal ashore, the six at table dined in a relaxed style foreign to the constraints of a long-haul flight. In the quiet seclusion of a taxi, returning well feasted through the darkened slumber of the island, our reality was none too hard to bear. *John Biscoe* was a homely home of sorts, and her lights were as welcoming as a lamp burning above a far-distant door.

* * *

Hanging above the dark recesses in the lower hold, the rigged clusters of bulbs illuminated the caverns of our continuing labours. It was a novelty for ship's staff to be joined by shore labour in loading the vessel with new cargo. It would devour her whole capacity to the brim. No space could be left unused. Observing the best principles of a tight stowage the local gang toiled with hundreds of food boxes, to fill the awkward and angular spaces in the wings. As tight as a fitted carpet, the oil drums were set upon their ends to fill the deck area. The dunnage of plywood sheets laid across their smooth expanse hid the lethal gaps between their rounded forms, where an unwary foot could plunge. On this crude and elevated floor the next tier of cargo was landed and variously dispersed. Despite precaution and the mutual protection of wary eyes, the workings of fate and coincidence brought their near misses.

As if to compensate in keeping up the numbers, John, the recently appointed environmental officer for the Survey, arrived aboard. Though sympathetic to accidents, his main concern was directed at the contents of any drums that passed through the ship's care. On a fact-finding mission, and to become more closely acquainted with his charges, he scrutinised warehouse and hold, and on the scientific bases probed the practices of managing pollution control. More used to casting a critical eye on the oil industry and patrolling the shores of distant Sullom Voe in the Shetland

Islands of the northern hemisphere, it was with a new relish that he brought his expertise to the far south.

The question hung unspoken in the air. It became a source of general interest, and despite the rain a small audience assembled with eyes lowered on to the tight stow of cargo. Would it all fit in? Planned to the last, the three huge crates spanned the width of the hatch opening. With the one-eyed squint of a surveyor peering through a theodolite, the clearance was judged between the guides of the heavy-cast beams. It would be a close thing. As the three beams were each swung and lowered, they dropped into place with a satisfying shudder. Narrow inches separated them from the cargo beneath. The moment brought its own justification. Nobody minded the final task of closing the hatch, wielding the wooden boards and tarpaulins, the locking bars and driven wooden wedges, to cover and protect the handiwork. We did not know then of the trials to which they would be subjected, as we all were, in the worst of sea crossings to regain Antarctic waters.

CHAPTER 6

Furthest South

*Fuel from the Soviets – the clutches of the Drake Passage – the magic of
Neumayer – Faraday revisited – Rothera – Greenpeace rendezvous –
an uncanny millpond – ceremonial at Port Stanley – a fitting departure.*

Departure brought with it a change in the routine course of events. At the
mouth of Port William, turning north instead of south happened rarely.
When it did occur it was significant – a mid-season break in Uruguay or
the start of a lengthy voyage on the return to Britain. Turning north on this
occasion was also important, but for the needs of the ship, not her crew.
Hugging the coast for the few miles into the adjacent Berkeley Sound,
bunkers were to be taken from a tanker anchored well up this substantial
inlet. A Soviet vessel, *Linkuva* by name, she was far from alone. Across the
intervening miles, binoculars brought to focus the shapes of other large
vessels. These were reefers, refrigerated ships chartered during the squid
fishing season to receive large catches from the many Japanese craft that
frequent Falkland waters.

    Linkuva was much in demand, a regular petrol pump for the commuting
traffic of shipping. The radio was busy with the complexities of arranging
times and quantities, all in a compromise of foreign languages. Their forms
small and dull on the horizon, the tanker's identity was guessed at rather
than known; cranes and derricks easily eliminated many from the contest.
The solitary posts at the centre to lift the umbilical pipework between ships
was sought, as was the telltale catwalk, the raised platform to carry feet
more easily over the labyrinth of pipelines on deck. I found my mark, and
with a yachtsman's ken adjusted the ship's head to the leeway of the strong

north wind. In crabwise fashion *John Biscoe* drew nearer her goal. It was another first: tying up alongside a Soviet ship.

With a curt efficiency towards safety they asked on our approach to switch off the radar. In the bitter wind and surging waves our pitching motion seemed not to be shared by the larger vessel. Berthing next to an anchored ship in jostling sea conditions was a different sensation to that of a quayside. The huge Yokohama balloon fenders afforded stout protection. The flinging of heaving lines was timed not only to distance but to the rise and fall of our bows. An urgency transmitted itself to get things right the first time. Heavily secured at last, the ropes slackened and tautened to the vagaries of our movement. The stresses and chafe some endured in the hours that followed were to keep the bosun's mate busy at a later date, in re-splicing new eyes. No shoelaces these, but hefty ropes requiring the seaman's craft to subdue and bend them to conform.

Hurled from the bridge-wing in defiance of the wind, the tightly rolled 'B' flag was caught on deck, then hoisted and broken out on the foremast. Red and swallow-tailed, it broadcast the etiquette of its message: loading dangerous goods. In settlement of the paperwork a representative was transferred between the ships. No red carpet or decorum for him, but an airy hoist on a man-lift of bridle ropes and a car tyre. His feet on its rim, and gripping the ropes, he smiled dubiously as the derrick wire whisked him aloft. From this dynamic and elevated perch he caught a unique glimpse of proceedings, though his thoughts were more inclined to the safety to be had on deck.

In three hours, 130 tons of fuel had been received. All was ready for departure. With propeller ever vulnerable to floating ropes, the small team at the stern played a rapid hand-over-hand tug of war, to bring in the trailing moorings more quickly than the stolid winch. Breathless, the advice was radioed to the bridge: 'All gone and clear aft.' No sooner was it spoken than the deck throbbed as propulsion was engaged. *Linkuva* was left to her lightened state as, with a seagoing trim, we headed rapidly down the sound. For our fuelling agent it was a day for arduous transfers. Once more in Port William, with a ladder rigged over the side, he descended to the waiting launch. It was to be an extraordinary and eventful period before we were to see him again.

Heading in our accustomed fashion south, the Falkland Islands were soon left behind. The northerly gale bore us with an invigorating scending motion, the following surf spreading wide at our sides in hissing swathes of white. It was the sound of a tall ship driven hard by a press of sail. In the darkness at handover, the chief officer and I compared notes on our experiences before the mast. Both trainees on the schooners of the Sail Training Association, the years dropped away with the recollections.

Lurking unseen, the eye of the depression hovered with an impressive tally of pressure; 940 millibars was a force to be reckoned with. The comfort of our passage was about to be lost. By morning, in the course of our combined movements, the wind had swung to the west and harried our flanks without mercy. We became resigned to yet another roller-coaster crossing of the Drake Passage. With a tight schedule, we pressed on, aiming for the Boyd Strait towards the western end of the South Shetland Islands.

Rolling with a stiff motion from the low-down weight of cargo and fuel, the drums at least seemed happy, heard to be creaking contentedly within their constraining chains. The fish were not so happy and caused grave concern to David, their keeper. Transferred live in ponds of polythene into temperature-controlled storage, the turmoil of their own tight world brought them major trauma. By comparison, my head cold was luxury. To endure it, together with the frenzied lurching of the ship, brought easy thoughts of becoming an ex-seafarer. In a mild delirium on the bunk, a fixation of the book cabinet above my feet springing from its fastenings to crush ribs did little to aid sleep. About the ship, references to 'only two weeks to go' were muttered in earnest. As the sun had crossed once more into the northern hemisphere and the days there advanced to meet the spring, it was a reflective and maverick little ship that headed south away from all such comforts.

Boyd Strait was a chaotic battleground for the conflicting humours of the elements, as if they did not quite know how to welcome *John Biscoe* once more into their midst. They offered threats of wind with white teeth, and a bluster of rolling clouds which enveloped the islands on either hand. The light ranged its emotions in subtle and intense moments of gloom and bright good cheer. Our own mood was sure; we had escaped the clutches of the Drake Passage. It was uplifting to feel the ship at her ease. As if in response, the weather relented and gave to the persevering the glimpses they sought. Smith Island raised her skirt to show a pale ankle of a snowy coast, while Low Island teased darkly from the horizon. At the Croker Passage, the chief officer's favourite flaunted curves of smooth ice and the spice of hard-edged bones of rock. Christiania Island had succumbed to his artist's eye; her features were well known to his pen and perceptions.

Across the smoothing waters where the Gerlache Strait begins, streamers of brash ice alluded to changes ahead. They were early messengers, as the broad highway of the strait was unadorned by icy attendants. Wrapped against the considerable chill in the evening warmth of colour, attending to the boats for their use on the next day afforded moments of reflection, appreciation at the timeless serenity of the bordering coasts and the unlooked-for pangs of wistful regret that such scenes would soon belong to my own past.

* * *

It was an act of faith to swing the ship boldly towards the high and unbroken frieze of mountains. Throughout the falling dusk a careful navigation had kept eyes averted from the scenic reality. There was some importance in finding the right gap, the entrance to the Neumayer Channel. The indented coast was interpreted on the radar screen; gleaned positions from the changing shapes of anticipated headlands were plotted on the chart. Through the near-blackness, the world had become painted as orange smudges on a glowing screen. From its eyes only would the entrance be found.

As concentration on a theme can stir the flash of memory – the stuff of experience to aid the present – I recalled in a passing instant the blackness of the Sound of Mull, a passage through Scottish islands with an entrance hidden in darkness. Yet the flash of Ardnamurchan Lighthouse and the promenade lights of Oban town helpfully mark its beginning and end. The Neumayer Channel was of a very different nature. Their similarity would cease beyond the miraculous fallback of land on either side, as an entrance was made.

The moment had arrived. 'Come easy to starboard now, on to 293 and she'll be nicely in line,' was the navigational advice I gave to the captain. Beyond the cold expanse of black windows, a defile lay in breathless silence, its headlands close on each side. In short minutes another substantial turn would bring us deep into its secretive domain. Assured of success, and in a moment to relax, the balcony of the bridge-wing offered a breath of fresh air and a spectacle to astonish. The fact that high and rugged terrain lay all about was known, and felt in its obscurity. On the instant of meeting the night air, there came a dwarfing enigma. Surely those suspended images were of ether, too fantastic to belong to earth! Like strange cloud patterns painted on canvas, the formations of crag and exposed rock hung at heights too high to seem credible. Elevating the gaze still further, in an undulating stratum ran snowy crests that touched the remnant of sky.

A pale light permeated all, startled by the piercing invasion of colour from the ship's sidelights; red and green were not natural here. The white of the masthead lights was more in keeping, and the frigid rod of the searchlight was of icy hue. Its unblinking gaze swung, as the tight turn swept us into the interior of the channel. Firmly in its grasp we probed onward with hushed awe. Underfoot lay a slush of snow. In the glassiness of utter calm, the dull reflections displayed their perfection. Lofty rock faces reached up from the water and marbled slopes were drawn as liquid curtains across the depths. Small bergs sat petrified in contemplation of their mirrored forms. On the radar screen tiny echoes moved at random, the trace of single birds in flight.

Across our path a mysterious and faint-lustred band leapt into brilliant intensity, caught in the advance of the searchlight beam. The brash ice kept close ranks, but its insubstantial mat cleaved with a brittle rasping. Zephyrs noiselessly brushed the face and dimpled the sea surface, erasing the delicate reflections and misting behind the veil of a more determined snowfall. Emerging from the central convolutions of the channel, in its broadening southern stretch the ship arrived at her anchorage. Close to Doumer Island, beyond the little lifeless base of Damoy, the shoal patch was approached with care. Its shallows are limited in extent: a useful summit on which to drop anchor. Too soon the echo sounder depths leaped to the desired figure, then slipped away. In such close confines reality outran the best-laid plans and the occasional shortcomings of our skills. With resignation the anchor was let go, and it found its own mark. It was no mean feat to traverse the inner reaches of this darkened byway. To await daylight brought a prudent pause and a sufficiency to the day.

Three months had passed since *John Biscoe*'s own particular Christmas. The twin peaks of Cap Renard heralded the beginning to my own new day. Their buxom loftiness thrust well beyond the overhang of the shelter deck. I had to stoop low to glimpse their tips. The Lemaire Channel showed another mood, with more concentration of ice than in previous passages. Into its inner recesses, bergs had groped and foundered. Beyond the discipline of their avoidance, in the limbo of clear waters it was refreshing to feel again the scale of our insignificance. Dwarfed on either side by walls rising almost sheer for 1,000 feet and more, we passed unnoticed in the timescale of their regard. Beyond, at the habitation of Faraday base, our arrival was anticipated.

The Meek Channel had effectively been blocked by a small berg, sealing off its reaches to all but the little inflatable boats which edged by with determination. The doorstep delivery was vital airfreight. By return came a bottle of sherry from the doctor, who was seemingly content in his new and exclusive practice.

A current of fresh anticipation found its release as we resumed our passage south. The destination was unusual for *John Biscoe*. The journey that ensued covered new ground for many, and a penetration well beyond the Antarctic Circle, to the much talked-of Rothera base on Adelaide Island. Navigation posed its problems in the long expanse of Grandidier

Channel. To one side lay the burgeoning coast of the Antarctic Peninsula. Hidden by an atmospheric veil, its glory was shrouded from eager eyes. We were privileged to have full measure and more on the return.

On the chart, the coasts were fringed by many blank spaces, hemmed in by hatched lines depicting the limits of surveys, enhancing their mystery still further. Scant and distant, to the other side tiny outcrops of known rocks were sought for visual comfort. Slyly awash, Grim Rocks were also eventually spotted, the dark curling cusp of a careless wave suddenly revealing its hideous threat. By evening, as the channel merged with Crystal Sound, the presence of ice grew ever more frequent at the northern cape of Adelaide Island. Between it and Liard Island lay another gateway into extremes. It led into Hanusse Bay and on to a notable constriction. The Gullet by name, it caused incredulous gulps at its darkened prospect. Beyond, the Barlas Channel connects to the wide expanse of Laubeuf Fjord, the spectacular environs of our destination.

Several tedious hours were to pass overnight before arrival at Rothera. It was not an extravagance to have both radar sets functioning. To one, with its observer's view forward into the searchlight beam and proximity of ship's controls, fell the task of detecting ice. On short range, these targets showed well, and a weaving course saw the passing of many pale forms close on either hand. Equally scrutinised, the other radar sought the wider view, to help keep track of our changing position in the scheme of land, islets and rocks. Deception was easy in the blackness. Near Hoodwink Island was a timely reminder to take nothing for granted. Seemingly grasping at straws along the coast of Liard Island, finally a glorious headland resolved itself into a point worthy of trust. For the return journey, beside its charted shape, the words were gratefully pencilled: good for navigation.

* * *

It was a navigator's reference, a meaningful position beyond its stark figures. At 67° 34'S, 68° 8'W, Rothera base is to be found. We were expected, yet our hosts were in a fluster at our singular arrival at their front gate. Lingering offshore in the growing light of morning, it was a scar on the pristine landscape that relentlessly fascinated and repelled the eye; Rothera was being 'developed'.

In the incongruous setting, the trappings of such activity could only be watched with uneasy or admiring wonder. Headlamps of huge vehicles busily swarmed along the artificial highway. Dumper trucks bore heavy loads of infill stone. Into the gaping void behind the new quay this aggregate was bulldozed and levelled. The tall and spindly-latticed arm of a crane swung as a baton to the discord of movement, silent at least to our own ears. Steel piles rose in a symmetry of unnatural geology. At its side a small tugboat lay tethered, a large barge moored nearby. The artificial plain of the aircraft runway stretched into the distance, leading the eye to the stepped townscape of the base and the quarters of the Canadian construction company.

Delicate and simple, a thin line of marker poles enticed the gaze aloft. Up this adjacent ice slope the old highway ran towards the former airstrip, with its foundation of ice rather than crushed stone. On the opposite craggy rise, a red-and-white windsock of vast dimension hung limp in the lifeless air. About the wider waters, ice fragments lay scattered in untidy profusion, 'like the aftermath of an explosion in a polystyrene factory'.

In preparation for our arrival, the east end of the quay had received frantic attention. It was to be a dishevelled christening of this new facility, but an event for the construction team; it was the icing on the cake of their endeavours to see the first ship berth. In some ways it seemed fitting that the role should fall to *John Biscoe*. There was approval that the quay be officially named after her.

The bulldozer found an alternative use. It provided a well-placed and immovable mooring point for two of the ship's ropes. Their eyes slipped round its beak-like hook, with a pneumatic power, it buried deep into the compacted surface of stone. The novelty of arrival was savoured in short-lived style. Soon, a pressing reality resumed. The clamour of activity struck harshly, immediate to our finely tuned senses. Cabin windows became filled with the sight of tumbling rock and the stolid advances of hardworking heavy plant. Compressors roared and pneumatic drills crackled. For the divers descending into the uncharacteristically grimy soup of water, however, this was a street scene of disrupted suburbia, viewed blankly from the ranks of a bus queue.

With a mild hypocrisy the mechanical conveniences were accepted, to ease the burden of our cargo work. In a relay, the shore crane paired with the movements of its smaller counterpart on the ship, linking our stern with the waiting trailers towards the bows. In the intervening space the skeleton structure of the quay lay exposed, a lattice of girders seeing their last of the sky. Soon they would be buried deep beneath a press of stone.

A maritime appendage added to the outskirts of this urban sprawl, and, contributing to its hectic pulse, *John Biscoe* seemed overtaken in her time. She belonged to quieter places, to simple technology and a scale of human endeavour more pioneering than dominating. The runway's straight certainty was a bold statement. Not all could view it with equanimity. To some it seemed the thin end of an undesirable wedge. There was a sense that perhaps something precious was being lost; it was the other side of progress.

The construction workers were provided with a temporary village of regimented flat-roofed buildings. Beyond these were to be found the huskies. A line of chains running across the stony levels served as a common tether. Each on its own lead, every dog had long since explored and accepted the circular limits of its constraint. The creatures were eagerly sought, promising the universal balm of canine companionship. Tackling the muddy scars of the building site, churned grey by tracks of vehicles, the dogs were found gazing reflectively towards the distant activity. A mechanical digger slowly pawed at a slope, dwarfed by a bay of bergs and a rearing ice shelf. Seemingly more abandoned than parked, on a flanking slope sat skidoos and a tracked snowcat, mere dots in comparison with the huge aircraft hangar and fuel tanks, and the horizontal enormity of the runway under construction. In greeting, the huskies endearingly wagged their tails and licked their paws.

Work aboard ship continued apace. In the depths of the lower hold a tight stow of heavy drums full of wastes slowly rose towards the 'tween deck opening, each layer separated by a wooden lattice of dunnage. It was filthy work that raised the customary ribbing to lighten the noisome, sweat-inducing toil. Both workplace and home, without the necessity of commuting, *John Biscoe* was ever a vessel of neighbouring contrasts. In only minutes the hold had been quitted for a hasty lunch break of a lamb joint, followed by gateau, eaten in the cabin's privacy. A Vivaldi cello concerto restored harmony against the reverberating discord on deck, and in the head.

The day of 29 March was a significant one. In the annals of *John Biscoe* it marked the beginning of her ultimate leave-taking from the Antarctic. From Rothera's farthest-south location her courses would be steadfastly towards the north. At the scientific base a token of the ship's visit had been gratefully received. A presentation plaque of *John Biscoe* would assume a particular poignancy.

The otherwise routine appearance of preparing to depart was lent a surreal aspect by the robotic and rhythmic clanging of a pile driver, as the ropes were released from the grip of the bulldozer. In the open water off the berth Captain Elliott contrived the ship's memorable farewell manoeuvre: 'It was the nautical equivalent of a flypast – and no less spectacular.' The spectre of a lingering mist tempered the homeward-bound sensation of the grand purpose newly embarked upon. The conduct of a lengthy and still-challenging voyage remained in the detail of each passing minute.

A day ahead of the itinerary, good speed was maintained up Laubeuf Fjord so as to make The Gullet before light failed. After tea my watch-keeping relief Graham made a request: 'I want no ice, no fog and no rocks at midnight.' He resigned himself to the retort, 'There's no harm in asking…'

The Antarctic is a clever mistress. Anxious to leave a favourable impression, what was denied us southbound was now paraded in intoxicating measure. A trump card of scenic effects had been reserved in Barlas Channel. Above low clouds, craggy peaks were sharp-edged against the sunset colours of sky; ahead was a radiant vista of white mountains. Darkness gave way to a lunar light. Bright to the full moon's face the illumined sides of tall bergs and brash ice showed a detail of forms. Their shadowed sides were dark and formless. A southerly breeze stirred a slight following sea to ripple the moon's broadening reflection on the unobstructed areas of water. The ship was transiting Crystal Sound in an erratic but careful zig-zagging of courses.

Come the morning the moon still presided, low in the west and opposing the blaze of sunrise, roseate tints warming the blue. The air was still. Hints of newly formed frazil ice had begun to touch the sea's surface with a harbinger of harsher climes. The calm conditions rendered the hazard of Grim Rock innocuous as it was easily sighted awash. At Faraday base a fresh fall of snow lay like a lace tablecloth set out in welcome for our arrival. Meek Channel heeded its name for the six hours *John Biscoe* was moored across its width. In parting, Faraday requested that a visual check be made on the tiny seasonal outpost of Damoy. Sailing plans were therefore modified away from the Gerlache Strait, for a return through the Neumayer Channel. Eventually pausing in Dorian Bay, a boat party was dispatched. Aided by a reluctant torch and moonlight, the bosun's mate ensured that the building that constitutes Damoy was given a security inspection.

Once again transiting Neumayer in darkness, heading northwards it was like a new entity, adding to the sense of isolation and the ever-present but mute imperative to get things right. The bold right-angle turn was drawing near. Once more the orange glow of the radar display enabled our passage, as the captain conned the manoeuvre: 'If you increase to starboard fifteen now, she should miss the ice…' The screen's speckling on the otherwise black of the channel betrayed loose ice. In stately arc the ship's bows swept the searchlight beam across the lurking threat, now thrown into dazzling reality as it passed harmlessly on the port side, Neumayer's own parting gift.

It was an emphatic issuing forth into the broader expanse of Gerlache Strait, and with it a sense of comparative ease. It lasted a few seconds and prompted an exclamation: 'A light! – is someone signalling us?'

The Chilean base at Waterboat Point. (Author's collection)

Having become so used to an almost complete absence of external aids to navigation, it was a comic irony to be thrown momentarily into confusion by such a facility. Lavtaro Island Light was seen to be dutifully flashing its signal every five seconds. Never before had it been observed working, and its charted symbol was all but disregarded. It blinked and receded astern. Bergy bits and growlers in the strait were reluctant to relinquish their assertive hold on a navigator's attention.

The ship's gloss surfaces were dulled with rime, a stealthy by-product of a chilling mist that greeted the dawn, as *John Biscoe* crossed Bransfield Strait bound for a special rendezvous at Deception Island. Fog obscured the approach but the first hint of land was a smooth snow slope seen above the layered blanket. We had been blessed with a weather portal, a miraculous clearing which revealed the geological stacks of Sewing Machine Needles and allowed for a spectacular re-entry into the cratered interior of Deception. In Whalers Bay two notable red-hulled ships were now at anchor, intent on a meeting. In the intense sunlight of noon, wrested from the gloom by the island's warming influence, rarely were their colours seen with such vivid clarity. *John Biscoe*'s traditional lines found counterpoint in the modern conversion of the Greenpeace polar campaign vessel *Gondwana*. Her role in the Antarctic included inspection of all scientific bases to assess environmental impact. Their unusual request had been supported by a compelling remark: 'Something has happened to the penguins.' A boat transfer brought dead penguin chicks found by

Greenpeace. The British Antarctic Survey had agreed to carry them back to Britain in the cold-rooms of *John Biscoe*, for analysis. Ashore, the evidence of the sustained efforts by the clean-up party also awaited transfer to the ship. In the old hangar many more drums of gleaned waste materials made up two large loads which topped up the hold to capacity.

The Drake Passage, testing arena of so many arduous crossings, was, on this occasion, like a millpond. The stillness was uncanny, lending credence to our fancy that the gods were smiling on our odyssey. We were tempted by the prospect of making a record crossing to the Falkland Islands, and the ship held a fine bone in her teeth up to the recognised finishing line off Cape Pembroke. The record was not broken but the joy was in the attempt. Advantage was also taken of the weather to begin smartening ship. *John Biscoe* was to be honoured with a special send-off from the Falklands, and eventually the whole ship would be painted on the voyage to Britain. It was good husbandry to prioritise the foreparts, before the headwinds of the north-east Trades would make mischief of the efforts.

John Biscoe's gambol on the racetrack advanced her scheduled arrival at Port Stanley to an uncivilised hour. Anchoring in Blanco Bay until '7-bells' breakfast was called, the captain casually proffered to the chief officer, 'Do you want to take her through the narrows?' With the imminence of a busy port call to orchestrate, the reply between close colleagues was humorously anticipated: 'Not particularly.'

A rendezvous with the Greenpeace ship *Gondwana* at Deception Island, to accept preserved penguin-chick carcases for analysis in Britain. (Author's collection)

As every event for the ship could now be labelled as 'final', those who had served for many years on *John Biscoe* would have their particular feelings of occasion and memory. It was evidently novel to berth the ship starboard side to the quay. The side opposite to the well-deck stowage of the piggybacked barge and launch, it enabled the unusual quantity of cargo to be efficiently offloaded, as well as the substantial backload which was to follow.

On the quayside, carriers postponed other tasks to attend to *John Biscoe*. Four flatbed articulated lorries were mobilised to take the hundreds of drums of waste. As if in early protest one of the ship's long-suffering cargo winches failed. There is never a good time for such an event. The frustrated wielding of heavy spanners and hammers found a steady build-up of stubby nuts and washers on the deck. The protective cover was removed to reveal a complexity of electrics and mechanisms. The expertise of Alan was called upon; a replacement part needed to be fabricated in his workshop. In the meantime one of the derricks was rigged to swing the cargo between the ship's hold and the quayside. A deal of teeth-gritting manual hauling found deck officer and radio officer alike teaming up for unaccustomed exercise. As the repaired winch was eventually reinstated the etiquette of gratitude was traditionally double-edged: 'Nice one Alan – what took you so long?'

None were displeased when the final layer of drums was reached. These were the worst of the slimy containers, painted with a gaudy graffiti: GASH DIESEL. Rank, and dank, the supporting wooden layer of dunnage was removed, and sawdust applied to the deck of the hold, prior to cleaning. The drums' final destinations were at hand, being variously sorted by contractors for dispatch to landfill, incineration or more specialist treatments.

Attention was turned to receiving new cargo. Once again the hold spaces were refreshed voids waiting to be filled. Opposite the ship the plucky little all-terrain vehicles had been running in neutral to dry out their fuel tanks before crating and re-stowing. An old tractor with seized steering became the latest toy for the chief officer to play with. Fulfilling the fantasy of a tank driver he guided the awkward machine by braking on individual wheels. Mudguards had been removed to avoid damage from the lifting strops. Excessively heavy for the ordinary cargo wire to lift, the derrick apparatus was 'doubled-up' in an act of traditional seamanship now largely read about only in classic maritime texts. So, too, was the low technology of battening down the wooden hatches, with its esoteric nomenclature of 'King' and portable beams, boards, tarpaulins, battens, wedges and locking bars.

The day of 5 April was special for a select few of the ship's company; it was the day their wives arrived. Like the spouses of many members of the armed forces, home life is sustained by these quietly resilient family members whose efforts can go unsung or unappreciated in their own communities. They are the invisible force behind any ship's crew, enabling the professional work to be achieved over the horizon. They have earned a collective official title – the Watch Ashore. In the coming weeks they cast new perspectives on daily events, fresh and enquiring eyes to appreciate and share what otherwise might have been taken for granted. *John Biscoe*'s senior master, Malcolm Phelps, also rejoined ship for the voyage home.

The prime task of loading cargo having been completed, plans for Sunday's official ceremony were set in motion. Across the air waves of Falklands Radio, Captain Elliott spoke with authority and warmth about *John Biscoe*, her wealth of associations with the islands and examples of extracurricular activities she willingly performed on behalf of remote off-island settlements. Under a crisp blue sky, crew took to the mastheads to dress ship overall with a painstakingly prepared fanfare of signal flags. Key areas of the ship were staged for the visitation of dignitaries. Uniforms were scrutinised.

The departure ceremony was to be an event of precision. It had been given an official time slot: 10.54 a.m. to 12.18 p.m. As *John Biscoe* quietly left her berth and crept up the harbour in brilliant sunshine, the stilled radar scanners offered no assistance in checking progress against the clock. Visual references with landmarks along Stanley's waterfront were the only guides. It was a profound observation by the captain as he fine-tuned the speeds: 'Time passes slowly; time passes quickly.' At precisely 11.30, head-to-wind and in line with the flag staff of Government House, *John Biscoe*'s Falkland Islands ensign was dipped. It was acknowledged by the governor's standard.

Gently churning the mud, a caramel trail in the otherwise blue testified to the shallow water in which the ship manoeuvred. The captain was pleased; planning and execution had brought the desired result. Relaxing for an instant over the bridge-wing, his exclamation came as a surprise: 'I don't believe it!' Crestfallen, he pointed at the old tyre fender still hanging mischievously over the side. Never mind, it was the beauty spot placed on the face of a much-loved film star.

Recovery was swift, as the smart launch *Warrah* came alongside. The governor and his wife, along with other dignitaries, boarded for formal entertainment in the wardroom, and to witness the eleven-gun salute from Victory Green. It was crowded with spectators; balloons and flares traced the sky. A cacophony of horns rent the air. Back in deeper water the *Warrah* led the flotilla in a full-speed flourish out through the narrows, *John Biscoe* keeping pace until obscured from the town. Lying quietly at anchor in the outer sound, the theatrical stage set could be dismantled. Some elements would see the light of day again at Montevideo.

The bosun, John, had been such an integral part of the life of *John Biscoe* for a score of years. He had been her head crewman. A native of the Falklands, he now stood on the foredeck in colourful going-ashore garb, chatting with his friends who were still very much in their working attire. At this moment he made his farewells and final leave-taking. Behind him the understanding of his colleagues remained unspoken, in the echoing corridors and convolutions of the vessel that had responded to his care.

* * *

John Biscoe left her anchorage in early afternoon, following the familiar graphite highway delineated on the navigational charts towards Montevideo. North-east of the Falklands, in the fall of dusk, the fleet of Japanese squid boats – last seen in Stanley renewing their fishing licences – switched on their working lights. They appeared as fluorescent strips, searing with a cold intensity. Later, their indirect looms glimmered as cold white fires over the horizon, before merging to a sky-brightness as significant as a rising moon on high cloud. *John Biscoe* had re-entered the world of shipping and shipping matters, of vessels that pass in the night with unpredictable human presence. With a niggling unease, the wilderness world of the Antarctic was now at our backs.

Fisheries patrol ship *Falklands Protector* arrives at Port Stanley after a tour of duty. (Author's collection)

Right: Bull elephant
seals sparring.
(Author's collection)

Below: The multi-
national scientific
complex at Fildes
Bay, South Shetlands.
(Author's collection)

Left: 'Smoko'. (Author's collection)

Below: Routine maintenance: 'turning over' a lifeboat engine. (Author's collection)

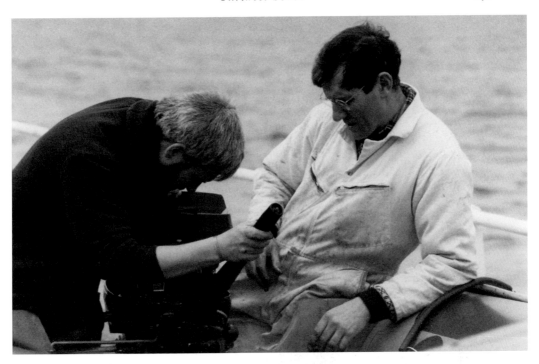

Mechanical problems exercise the chief officer, and chief engineer, Simon Taylor. (Author's collection)

Alan Jones: a one-man bespoke card factory. (Author's collection)

CHAPTER 7

A Flourishing Finale

Passage to Britain – a right 'royal' welcome.

The passage to Montevideo assumed the air of a working holiday. The fine conditions and steady rise in temperature enabled those with moments of leisure to indulge in sun worship. The returning scientists were good-naturedly press-ganged into useful service. They were glad at the opportunity of gainful exercise in the fresh air, as they tackled rust stains on the white gloss-work and spruced up the finish to the teak decks. Attention was briefly directed back to Antarctica by a radio call. The Dutch vessel *Prinsengracht* was currently bound for Rothera, scheduled to arrive eight days hence. Informed of the ice conditions we had encountered, her own progress into a maturing polar autumn could be envisioned, a contrast with our own kindlier circumstances.

On arrival off Montevideo, the status of our little ship was reaffirmed by the larger-than-life pilot. Dressed in a pale suit which deepened further his impressive countenance, on gaining the bridge he pronounced, 'My name is Carrosa; Winston Carrosa – after your Churchill, captain. I was born in 1942. *John Biscoe* – ah! This ship come many many years; all people know...'

Montevideo was enjoyed as home for some, with visits by family, or explored as a last opportunity. Replenished for what was to be a twenty-six-day direct run back to England, *John Biscoe* backed out of her berth, discreetly except for the warning signal of three blasts on her siren. Those not travelling onward gave poignant waves from the vacant dockside.

The next four days found the ship coasting the continental waters, slowly trending away on a leg of 1,000 miles. Protective canvas covers were removed from air vents, previously vulnerable to damp and deluge by seas. Lack of air conditioning in the accommodation brought an interior humidity that rendered surfaces clammy. External doors were secured open, and the burgeoning heat encouraged groups to gather on the decks or hatch covers, places of companionable evening leisure, latterly more accustomed to frigid desolation. On the after deck, so often a workplace of ardent endeavour by fisheries scientists in their trawl-sampling of Southern Ocean marine life, spangles of coloured lights effectively dispelled the demons of toil.

In the mornings the scientists queued at the paint locker door forward. In motley working gear they were issued with paint, brushes, and instructions: white bulwarks, cutting in with black. The anchoring windlass was attended by a cheery party. Fussing at the old tarpaulin which protected the deck, they attacked the complex machinery with enthusiasm, assuming balletic poses and recumbent attitudes to reach their goals. Others took guidance from crew, in the more technical maintenance of cargo pulleys, able to lift their eyes to appreciate the silvery darts of flying fish that sailed to freedom away from our bows.

Those with a bent for mathematics, or a simple romance of the sea, caused a resurgence of interest in navigation. As ever the working use of sextants generated awe. Beyond the bows the panoply of stars gained in recognition with each passing night. Near to the horizon an 'upside-down' Plough seemed impossibly big in the sky. The two pointers to the Pole Star hinted at Polaris, as yet well beyond sight. Gradually the Plough, envoy of the north, rose as others to the south dipped and left us. That constellation slowly cartwheeled one-handed across the invisible horizon, daily becoming more acrobatic as it reached ever higher in the celestial dome.

For a vessel more used to a frequency of manoeuvring during her daily round, having only three nominal courses to follow for little short of 6,000 miles would come either as a rest or monotony for the steering systems. Saving the logged manual tests during each watch the auto-helm kept the required headings, subject only to minor adjustments and avoidance of encountered shipping. The new course was an ocean leap towards the Cape Verde Islands, and would take *John Biscoe* not only across the equator but well into the northern hemisphere. In a matter of days she was to leave a second continent and seek out that of Africa.

As longitude decreased, ship's clocks were advanced. A barbeque was held on deck. Cousins of the northern gannet, boobies squawked teasingly in flight, diving and chasing flying fish on the surface. We learnt that the ship visiting Rothera had left after working round-the-clock for three days, to escape the insidious clutches of the season.

Dwarfed beneath the open canopy of an oceanic sky, the march of towering nimbus clouds and their trailing skirts of rain could be seen and monitored, even dodged, to preserve freshly applied paintwork. Some were too vast. Before an onslaught, the horizon would lower, and squalls menaced the sea. Engineers on watch below were warned to close the engine-room skylights. Radar screens became electronically blotted, and, as visibility was obliterated by the amorphous monster, wiper blades started their rhythmic beat to the purr of drive motors, and the whirring clear-view screen flung drops asunder, like a sparkling Catherine wheel. The scuppers gurgled like a downpipe outside a cottage kitchen door. The downpours brought a welcome coolness. In the aftermath, with a reappearance of the sun, a refreshed normality resumed.

A lengthy uninterrupted voyage to some enquiring passengers promotes an active interest and participation in aspects of shipboard life. On *John Biscoe*, the do-it-yourself satisfaction of home improvements was evident in the ever-smartening exterior. A few wished to try their hand at steering the ship: after all, 'how hard could it be?' They soon found out. Presented with the challenge of achieving the Steering Certificate required as a recognised basic qualification for junior crew, several of the scientists undertook the training.

Assigned hourly 'tricks at the wheel', each had their initial confidence shattered. Advised of the course to steer, when given manual control all was well for a few seconds, after which time the turning of the wheel left and right became progressively more animated and frantic. Composure vanished; panic showed in raised complexions and beads on the brow. The ship had become like a thing possessed, lurching from side to side in a widening zigzag any hunting submarine commander would despair at. It was a harsh lesson, one to which all cocky initiates are subjected. No, steering a ship is nothing like driving a car.

Over the following days, the trainees gradually got to grips with the simplest task of maintaining a steady course in the open sea. Gradually introduced to the terms, etiquette and execution of helm orders for manoeuvring, the satisfaction of seeing new skills develop was shared equally by the person at the helm and the watch-keeping officer.

In the course of *John Biscoe*'s final voyage north from Rothera, she crossed the latitudes of the Antarctic Circle and the two tropics, as well as the longitude of the prime meridian. At half-past midnight on 23 April, she crossed perhaps the most celebrated of them all. In advance of the equator, the doldrums – notorious of sailing-ship days – duly held their breath in a windless calm. Low swells persisted, residual from the south-east, but with them came a hint of movement from another direction. Felt beneath the feet rather than observed, it subtly lifted our bows. Herald of her own trade winds, we were beckoned onwards into the northern hemisphere.

In the run of events, *John Biscoe* may well have crossed the equator seventy times on her annual return migrations between Britain and Antarctica. On each of these the time-honoured ceremony of 'Crossing the Line' would have been enacted by successions of experienced crews, and 'first-timers' subjected to the rigours of theatrically paying homage to King Neptune and his Queen. Tradition demanded it, but at a civilised hour: after lunch. The victims were brought before the court, to be automatically pronounced 'very guilty' on trumped-up charges. They suffered contrived humiliations in the interests of justice – and of fun; it involved leftover food scraps and dowsing with hoses. It was a privilege for them, delayed in the appreciation, to be issued with certificates on this, the ultimate such ceremony on *John Biscoe*.

Midway between the continents of South America and Africa, temperatures reassuringly dropped by several degrees. It brought sundry comforts: the fourth engineer was able to add a touch of hot to his shower water; the midnight watchman resumed wearing a tee-shirt; crew could quit night-time sleeping on the hatch tops and avoid the attentions of a waxing moon; and slumber could once more be taken pleasurably under a duvet. Freak atmospheric conditions affecting radio waves carried sporadic VHF signals from marine stations off western Africa, artificially shrinking our isolation from the wider world. Solid ground appeared in the distant forms of the Cape Verde Islands. A logbook entry recorded the significant waypoint for alteration on to the last great leg of the journey: Pta Mangrade Light 108° x 8 miles.

The first day of May brought rumour to the breakfast table that Madeira was in the offing. Viewing an empty horizon over the rim of a mug of coffee, the mischievous electrician quizzed, 'So where's Madeira then?' He could anticipate the riposte: 'Surely you don't want your sherry already?' West of the island, a change of wind was also to mark a change in the fortunes of the voyage, confirming the wearisome law of 'so near yet so far'. Areas of high pressure are generally greeted as benign entities, meteorological phenomena opposed to the traits of depressions. As with good intentions everywhere, there can be a downside. *John Biscoe* found herself ill placed, as a large anticyclone was nestling down for an intensifying stay to the north-west of us, and the prospect of contrary winds.

The depletion of food stocks became noticeable; it was nothing to challenge the reserves, but potatoes, butter, sugar, cheese and cereals had all been popular. As the major consumables of engine fuel and fresh water rendered various tanks empty, the ship's draught and trim were affected. To maintain good sea-keeping qualities, particularly against the unwelcome head seas, the substantial after peak tank at the stern was filled with seawater ballast, increasing the hull's grip in the water and enabling the bows to ride more kindly over the advancing ranks of waves. The seas grew in stature. In response the ship's speed was decreased for comfort: 8; 7; 6 knots. Battening down included re-covering vulnerable deck ventilators and checking the security of the cargo hatch. Inside individual cabins, tracking down rolling batteries and toiletries in drawers became a social imperative, to cease their clanking in the night.

Keen on a bucking-bronco experience, scientists braved the bridge-wings, ducking their tanned faces below the dodgers, away from the stinging caress of the spray which encrusted even the funnel with salt. On a level with Lisbon, the first distant sighting of a bright white northern gannet briefly recalled the southern boobies, then more strongly the great island colonies of Britain: Ailsa Craig and Bass Rock, not far from home. In such a fleeting moment, Planet Earth can be rendered small, yet the purgatory of clawing relentlessly against the weather also made it an ironic notion.

Ease came from an unlikely source: the Bay of Biscay. It was careless of its reputation. Our crossing towards Ushant – the real and psychological turning point into the English Channel – was a welcome reward. Entering the lengthy maritime slipstream which eventually carries commercial shipping to and from the busiest bottleneck in the world, the Dover Straits, the increasing congestion of these near-Continental waters came as a wake-up call to particular watch-keeping skills, skills that had lain largely dormant when in seas devoid of other human activity. With them came requirements of obligatory reporting to monitoring shore stations.

Suddenly within proper VHF range, the prospect dawned of being able to make radio link calls to home. None begrudged the £5 charge for a three-minute communication. Kept brief and matter-of-fact, constrained by the knowledge that they were transmitted across the open airwaves, nevertheless the voices of loved ones broke a spell. Time had passed slowly; now it started to pass quickly. As proximity to home had been undeniably revealed, thoughts turned to packing up not only each individual's possessions, but the removal of many ship's items, which would remain property of the British Antarctic Survey.

In the bridge drawers, accustomed to only a few ocean charts, which had registered each day's progress in hops of inches, suddenly a bulk of Channel and local charts appeared. Displaying the graphic plans of the ship's navigator up to the Humber pilot station, they bore testimony to the rapid unfolding of coastal navigation. Hanging on a clipboard above the chart table, a neat tabulated abstract listed the romantic-sounding names of waymarks for the remaining legs of the passage: Channel light vessel; Bassurelle; Vergoyer North; Varne; Sandettie light vessel; East Goodwin; Drill Stone; Orfordness; NE Cross Sands Buoy; East Sheringham Buoy; South Race Buoy; North Race Buoy; and finally, Spurn Head pilot station.

The unbidden glance can often bring the best surprise. It was in the early evening of the penultimate day that a casual eye to the north gave the first glimpse of England's shore: an undulating line of pale pewter, sandwiched between the silvery greys of a spring sky and a beside-the-seaside sea.

* * *

A freshly sharpened pencil was used to make the final entry into the navigation workbook: 'May 8th 1991: Humber estuary – Grimsby approach: 10.36 a.m. End of Passage off Spurn Head: Total distance 6,314 nautical miles.' The remaining miles from embarking the pilot to the berth at Grimsby docks were recorded as 'Harbour Steaming'. The River Humber showed the kindly face of another fine spring morning, its familiar silt-laden stream completing the circle of a voyage that had begun in the bronzed estuarial waters of South America's mighty River Plate.

In contrast to the flamboyant Latin pilot of Montevideo, the present incumbent displayed the competent reserve of his native county. Beneath the celebrated brick edifice of Grimsby's hydraulic tower, the curved arm of the dock approach invited *John Biscoe* out of the running tide. At high water slack, arrival was timed perfectly to pass straight through the opened lock into the tidal basin beyond. As she made stately progress towards the special berth, reserved for the official reception by the townsfolk, *Bransfield* – last seen in the Falklands – saluted with raucous fanfare.

In the upper reaches of the docks, Captain Phelps deftly pirouetted the ship in a flourishing finale to his command, her bows once more pointing seawards. The band of the Fleet Air Arm trumpeted her arrival. As the gleaming black limousine of the mayor's office added formality alongside the blue-and-white marquee, the throng of dignitaries, guests, families and well-wishers enlivened the occasion in the best traditions of an English garden party. For backdrop, the little ship whose illustrious career had, all of a sudden, come to a close. Speeches, presentations and newspaper headlines were made. Like a decorated Christmas tree, *John Biscoe* was the hub of attention, her flags and lengthy paying-off pennant fluttering contentedly in the balmy breeze. Beyond the ceremony the sign 'Ship for Sale' loomed large. It seemed unthinkable.

Eventually left in her lay-up berth, *John Biscoe* – with her extraordinary million miles – was left alone with the memory of her real home: the Antarctic.

Centre of attention! This was *John Biscoe*'s fitting welcome ceremony on her return to Grimsby, her home port in Britain. (Photo by *Scunthorpe Evening Telegraph*)

Unloading cargo on to the ice at Stonington Island with dogs and sleds, 1969/70. (Photo by M. G. White/BAS)

Acknowledgements

The author gratefully acknowledges with his thanks:-

Munro Sievwright and Alan Coley, respective personnel managers at the British Antarctic Survey and Research Vessel Services, for enabling me to serve on *John Biscoe*;

The ship's company aboard *John Biscoe* for their patience in being the scrutinised subject for both camera and notebook throughout the voyage;

Maurice O'Donnell, *John Biscoe's* radio officer, for initially typing much of the early text on the ship's old-fashioned typewriter;

Alan Jones, *John Biscoe's* electrical engineer, for his incisive caricature of the author;

Captain Chris Elliott, for providing an authoritative introduction to set *John Biscoe* in her proper historical context;

My wife Karen, for proof-reading the text, providing computer expertise, and for being an exemplary member of The Watch Ashore throughout my sea-going career;

The archive department of the British Antarctic Survey.

About the Author

Trevor Boult is an officer in the UK Merchant Navy and a freelance photo-journalist with a particular interest in maritime heritage subjects. He is regularly published in the maritime press.

Captain Elliott

Captain Chris Elliott joined the British Antarctic Survey as Third Officer on *John Biscoe* in 1967. Rising through the ranks, he was promoted Master in 1975. He served as Master for thirty years, the first fifteen years in command of *John Biscoe*, during which time the successful Offshore Biological Programme was established. A recipient of the Polar Medal in 1986, he was awarded the MBE in 2006 'For Services to Scientific Exploration and Maritime Operations in Polar Regions'. Elliott Passage, which runs between Adelaide Island and Jenny Island in Antarctica, was named after him.